Memoirs of Mary Robinson, "Perdita"

Mary Robinson

Edited by M. E. Robinson
and J. Fitzgerald Molloy

MEMOIRS

OF

MARY ROBINSON

"PERDITA"

FROM THE EDITION EDITED BY HER DAUGHTER

WITH INTRODUCTION AND NOTES BY

J. FITZGERALD MOLLOY

AUTHOR OF "THE LIFE AND ADVENTURES OF EDMUND
KEAN," "COURT LIFE BELOW STAIRS," &c.

WITH PORTRAITS

1895

Mrs Robinson.
from an Engraving by Smith, after Romney

INTRODUCTION TO THE ORIGINAL EDITION

he following brief Memoirs of a beautiful, engaging, and, in many respects, highly gifted woman require little in the way of introduction. While we may trace some little negative disengenuousness in the writer, in regard to a due admission of her own failings, sufficient of uncoloured matter of fact remains to show the exposed situation of an unprotected beauty–or, what is worse, of a female of great personal and natural attraction, exposed to the gaze of libertine rank and fashion, under the mere nominal guardianship of a neglectful and profligate husband. Autobiography of this class is sometimes dangerous; not so that of Mrs. Robinson, who conceals not the thorns inherent in the paths along which vice externally scatters roses. For the rest, the arrangement of princely establishments in the way of amour is pleasantly portrayed in this brief volume, which in many respects is not without its moral. One at least is sufficiently obvious, and it will be found in the cold-hearted neglect which a woman of the most fascinating mental and personal attractions may encounter from those whose homage is merely sensual, and whose admiration is but a snare.

EDITOR'S PREFACE.

HE author of these Memoirs, Mary Robinson, was one of the most prominent and eminently beautiful women of her day. From the description she furnishes of her personal appearance we gather that her complexion was dark, her eyes large, her features expressive of melancholy; and this verbal sketch corresponds with her portrait, which presents a face at once grave, refined, and charming. Her beauty, indeed, was such as to attract, amongst others, the attentions of Lords Lyttelton and Northington, Fighting Fitzgerald, Captain Ayscough, and finally the Prince of Wales; whilst her talents and conversation secured her the friendship and interest of David Garrick, Richard Brinsley Sheridan, Charles James Fox, Joshua Reynolds, Arthur Murphy, the dramatist, and various other men of distinguished talent.

Though her Memoirs are briefly sketched, they are sufficiently vivid to present us with various pictures of the social life of the period of which she was the centre. Now we find her at the Pantheon, with its coloured lamps and brilliant music, moving amidst a fashionable crowd, where large hoops and high feathers abounded, she herself dressed in a habit of pale pink satin trimmed with sable, attracting the attention of men of fashion. Again she is surrounded by friends at Vauxhall Gardens, and barely escapes from a cunning plot to abduct her–a plot in which loaded pistols and a waiting coach prominently figure; whilst on another occasion she is at Ranelagh, where, in the course of the evening, half a dozen gallants "evinced their attentions"; and ultimately she makes her first appearance as an actress on the stage of Drury Lane before a brilliant house, David Garrick, now retired, watching her from the orchestra, whilst she played Juliet in pink satin richly spangled with silver, her head ornamented with white feathers.

The fact of her becoming an actress brought about the turning-point in her life; it being whilst she played Perdita in The Winter's Tale before royalty that she attracted the Prince of Wales, afterwards George IV., who was then in his eighteenth year. The incidents which followed are so briefly treated in the Memoirs that explanations are necessary to those who would follow the story of her life.

The performance of the play in which the Prince saw her, probably for the first time, took place on the 3rd of December, 1779. It was not until some months later, during which the Prince and Perdita corresponded, that she consented to meet him at Kew, where his education was being continued and strict guard kept upon his conduct. During 1780 he urged his father to give him a commission in the army, but, dreading the liberty which would result from such a step, the King refused the request. It was, however, considered advisable to provide the Prince with a small separate establishment in a wing of Buckingham House; this arrangement taking place on the 1st of January, 1781.

Being now his own master, the Prince became a man about town, attended routs, masquerades, horseraces, identified himself with politicians detested by the King, set up an establishment for Mrs. Robinson, gambled, drank, and in a single year spent ten thousand pounds on clothes. He now openly appeared in the company of Perdita at places of public resort and amusement; she, magnificently dressed, driving a splendid equipage which had cost him nine hundred guineas, and surrounded by his friends. We read that—" To-day she was a *paysanne* with her straw hat tied at the back of her head. Yesterday she perhaps had been the dressed belle of Hyde Park, trimmed, powdered, patched, painted to the utmost power of rouge and white lead; to-morrow she would be the cravated Amazon of the riding house; but, be she what she might, the hats of the fashionable promenaders swept the ground as she passed."

This life lasted about two years, when just as the Prince, on his coming of age, was about to take possession of Carlton House, to receive £30,000 from the nation towards paying his debts, and an annuity of £63,000, he absented himself from Perdita, leaving her in ignorance of the cause of his change, which was none other than an interest in Mrs. Grace Dalrymple Elliott.

In the early fervour of his fancy he had assured Mrs. Robinson his love would remain unchangeable till death, and that he would prove unalterable to his Perdita through life. Moreover, his generosity being heated by passion, he gave her a bond promising to pay her £20,000 on his coming of age.

On the Prince separating from her, Perdita found herself some £7,000 in debt to tradespeople who became clamorous for their money, whereon she wrote to her royal lover, who paid her no heed; but presently she was visited by his friend, Charles James Fox, when she agreed to give up her bond in consideration of receiving an annuity of £500 a year.

She would now gladly have gone back to the stage, but that she feared the hostility of public opinion. Shortly after she went to Paris, and on her return to England devoted herself to literature. It was about this time she entered into relations with Colonel– afterwards Sir Banastre–Tarleton, who was born in the same year as herself, and had served in the American army from 1776 until the surrender of Yorktown, on which he returned to England. For many years he sat in Parliament as the representative of Liverpool, his native town; and in 1817 he gained the grade of Lieutenant-General, and was created a baronet. His friendship with Mrs. Robinson lasted some sixteen years.

It was whilst undertaking a journey on his behalf, at a time when he was in pecuniary difficulties, that she contracted the illness that resulted in her losing the active use of her lower limbs. This did not prevent her from working, and she poured out novels, poems, essays on the Condition of Women, and plays. A communication written by her to John Taylor, the proprietor of the *Sun* newspaper and author of various epilogues, prologues, songs, &c., gives a view of her life. This letter, now published for the first time, is contained in the famous Morrison collection of autograph letters, and is dated the 5th of October, 1794.

"I was really happy to receive your letter. Your silence gave me no small degree of uneasiness, and I began to think some *demons* had broken the links of that chain which I trust has united us in *frienship* for ever. Life is such a scene of trouble and disappointment that the sensible mind can ill endure the loss of any consolation that renders it supportable. How, then, can it be possible that we should resign, without a severe pang, the first of all human blessings, the friend we love? Never give me reason again, I conjure you, to suppose you have wholly forgot me.

"Now I will impart to you a secret, which must not be revealed. I think that before the 10th of December next I shall quit England *for ever* My dear and valuable brother, who is now in Lancashire, wishes to persuade me, and the unkindness of the *world* tends not a little to forward his hopes. I have no relations in England except my darling girl, and, I fear, few friends. Yet, my dear Juan, I shall feel a very severe struggle in quitting those paths of fancy I have been childish enough to admire–false prospects. They have led me into the vain expectation that fame would attend my labours, and my country be my pride. How have I been treated? I need only refer you to the critiques of last month, and you will acquit me of unreasonable instability. When I leave England–*adieu* to the *muse* for *ever*–I will never publish another line while I exist, and even those manuscripts now finished I WILL DESTROY.

"Perhaps this will be no loss to the world, yet I may regret the many fruitless hours I have employed to furnish occasions for malevolence and persecution.

"In every walk of life I have been equally unfortunate, but here shall end my complaints.

"I shall return to St. James's Place for a few days this month to meet my brother, who then goes to York for a very short time, and after his return (the end of November) I DEPART. This must be *secret* for to my other misfortunes pecuniary derangement is not the least. Let common sense judge how I can subsist upon £500 a year, when my carriage (a necessary expense) alone costs me £200. My mental labours have failed through the dishonest conduct of my publishers. My works have sold handsomely, but the profits have been theirs.

"Have I not reason to be disgusted when I see him to whom I ought to look for better fortune lavishing favours on unworthy objects, gratifying the *avarice of ignorance and dulness,* while I, who sacrificed reputation, an advantageous profession, friends, patronage, the brilliant hours of youth, and the conscious delight of correct conduct, am condemned to the scanty pittance bestowed on every indifferent page who holds up his ermined train of ceremony?

"You will say, ' Why trouble me with all this? ' I answer, ' Because when I am *at peace* you may be in possession of my real sentiments and defend my cause when I shall not have the power of doing it.'

"My comedy has been *a* long in the hands of manager, but whether it will ever be brought forward time must decide. You know, my dear friend, what sort of authors have lately been patronised by managers; their pieces ushered to public view, with all the advantages of splendour; yet I am obliged to wait two long years without a single hope that a trial would be granted. Oh, I am TIRED OF THE WORLD and all its mortifications. I promise you this shall close my *chapters of complaints* Keep them, and remember how ill I have been treated."

Eight days later she wrote to the same friend:

"In wretched spirits I wrote you last week a most melancholy letter. Your kind answer consoled me. The balsam of pure and disinterested friendship never fails to cure the mind's sickness, particularly when it proceeds from disgust at the ingratitude of the world."

The play to which she referred was probably that mentioned in the sequel to her Memoirs, which was unhappily a failure. It is notable that the principal character in the farce was played by Mrs. Jordan, who was later to become the victim of a royal prince, who left her to die in poverty and exile.

The letter of another great actress, Sarah Siddons, written to John Taylor, shows kindness and compassion towards Perdita.

"I am very much obliged to Mrs. Robinson," says Mrs. Siddons, "for her polite attention in sending me her poems. Pray tell her so with my compliments. I hope the poor, charming woman has quite recovered from her fall. If she is half as amiable as her writings, I shall long for the *possibility* of being acquainted with her. I say the *possibility* because one's whole life is one continual sacrifice of inclinations, which to indulge, however laudable or innocent, would draw down the malice and reproach of those prudent people who never do ill, ' but feed and sleep and do observances to the stale ritual of quaint ceremony.' The charming and beautiful Mrs. Robinson: I pity her from the bottom of my soul. "

Almost to the last she retained her beauty, and delighted in receiving her friends and learning from them news of the world in which she could no longer move. Reclining on her sofa in the little drawing-room of her house in St. James's Place she was the centre of a circle which comprised many of those who had surrounded her in the days of her brilliancy, amongst them being the Prince of Wales and his brother the Duke of York.

Possibly, for the former, memory lent her a charm which years had not utterly failed to dispel.

August 1894.   J. F. M.

LIST OF PLATES.

MRS. ROBINSON.
From an Engraving by J. R. Smith, after Romney.

MRS. ROBINSON.
Engraved by Roffe, after Cosway.

MRS. ROBINSON.
Engraved by Roffe, after Cosway.

MRS. ROBINSON.
From the Engraving by Dickenson, after Reynolds.

DUCHESS OF DEVONSHIRE.
From the Engraving by Bartolozzi, after J. Nixon.

MISS FARREN.
From the Engraving by Knight, after Lawrence.

MRS. ROBINSON AND THE PRINCE OF WALES.
From the Engravings by Sherwin and Burke.

MRS. ROBINSON.
From the Engraving by Daniell, after Dance.

MRS. ROBINSON.
From the Engraving by Burke, after Reynolds.

Melania
(Mrs Lawrence)

MEMOIRS

OF

MARY ROBINSON.

t the period when the ancient city of Bristol was beseiged by Fairfax's army, the troops being stationed on a rising ground in the vicinity of the suburbs, a great part of the venerable minster was destroyed by the cannonading before Prince Rupert surrendered to the enemy; and the beautiful Gothic structure, which at this moment fills the contemplative mind with melancholy awe, was reduced to but little more than one-half of the original fabric. Adjoining to the consecrated hill, whose antique tower resists the ravages of time, once stood a monastery of monks of the order of St. Augustine. This building formed a part of the spacious boundaries which fell before the attacks of the enemy, and became a part of the ruin, which never was repaired or re-raised to its former Gothic splendours.

On this spot was built a private house, partly of simple, and partly of modern architecture. The front faced a small garden, the gates of which opened to the Minster Green (now called the College Green); the west side was bounded by the cathedral, and the back was supported by the ancient cloisters of St. Augustine's monastery. A spot more calculated to inspire the soul with mournful meditation can scarcely be found amidst the monuments of antiquity.

In this venerable mansion there was one chamber whose dismal and singular constructure left no doubt of its having been a part of the original monastery. It was supported by the mouldering arches of the cloisters, dark, Gothic, and opening on the minster sanctuary, not only by casement windows that shed a dim mid-day gloom, but by a narrow winding staircase, at the foot of which an iron-spiked door led to the long gloomy path of cloistered solitude. This place

1

remained in the situation in which I describe it in the year 1776, and probably may, in a more ruined state, continue so to this hour.

In this awe-inspiring habitation, which I shall henceforth denominate the Minster House, during a tempestuous night, on the 27th of November, 1758, I first opened my eyes to this world of duplicity and sorrow. I have often heard my mother say that a more stormy hour she never remembered. The wind whistled round the dark pinnacles of the minster tower, and the rain beat in torrents against the casements of her chamber. Through life the tempest has followed my footsteps, and I have in vain looked for a short interval of repose from the perseverance of sorrow.

In the male line I am descended from a respectable family in Ireland, the original name of which was MacDermott. From an Irish estate, my great-grandfather changed it to that of Darby. My father, who was born in America, was a man of strong mind, high spirit, and great personal intrepidity. Many anecdotes, well authenticated, and which, being irrefragable, are recorded as just tributes to his fame and memory, shall, in the course of these memoirs, confirm this assertion.

My mother was the grandchild of Catherine Seys, one of the daughters and co-heiresses of Richard Seys, Esq., of Boverton Castle, in Glamorganshire. The sister of my great-grandmother, named Anne, married Peter, Lord King, who was nephew, in the female line, to the learned and truly illustrious John Locke–a name that has acquired celebrity which admits of no augmented panegyric.

Catherine Seys was a woman of great piety and virtue–a character which she transferred to her daughter, and which has also been acknowledged as justly due to her sister Lady King. [1] She quitted this life when my grandmother was yet a child, leaving an only daughter, whose father also died while she was in her infancy. By this privation of paternal care my grandmother became the élève of her mother's father, and passed the early part of her life at the family castle in Glamorganshire. From this period till the marriage of my mother I can give but a brief account. All I know is, that my grandmother, though wedded unhappily, to the latest period of her existence was a woman of amiable and simple manners, unaffected piety, and exemplary virtue. I remember her well; and I speak not only from report, but from my own knowledge. She died in the year 1780.

My grandmother Elizabeth, whom I may, without the vanity of consanguinity, term a truly good woman, in the early part of her life devoted much of her time to botanic study. She frequently passed many successive months with Lady Tynt, of Haswell, in Somersetshire, who was her godmother, and who was the Lady Bountiful of the surrounding villages. Animated by so distinguished an example, the young Elizabeth, who was remarkably handsome, [1] took particular delight in visiting the old, the indigent, and the infirm, resident within many miles of Haswell, and in preparing such medicines as were useful to the maladies of the peasantry. She was the village doctress, and, with her worthy godmother, seldom passed a day without exemplifying the benevolence of her nature.

My mother was born at Bridgwater, in Somersetshire, in the house near the bridge, which is now occupied by Jonathan Chub, Esq., a relation of my beloved and lamented parent, and a gentleman who, to acknowledged worth and a powerful understanding, adds a superior claim to attention by all the acquirements of a scholar and a philosopher.

My mother, who never was what may be called a handsome woman, had nevertheless, in her youth, a peculiarly neat figure, and a vivacity of manner which obtained her many suitors. Among others, a young gentleman of good family, of the name of Storr, paid his addresses. My father was the object of my mother's choice, though her relations rather wished her to form a matrimonial alliance with Mr. S. The conflict between affection and duty was at length decided in favour of my father, and the rejected lover set out in despair for Bristol. From thence, in a few days after his arrival, he took his passage in a merchantman for a distant part of the globe; and from that hour no intelligence ever arrived of his fate or fortune. I have often heard my mother speak of this gentleman with regret and sorrow.

My mother was between twenty and thirty years of age at the period of her marriage. The ceremony was performed at Dunyatt, in the county of Somerset. My father was shortly after settled at Bristol, and during the second year after their union a son was born to bless and honour them. [1]

Three years after my mother gave birth to a daughter, named Elizabeth, who died of the small-pox at the age of two years and ten months. In the second winter following this event, which deeply afflicted the most affectionate of parents, I was born. She had afterwards two sons: William, who died at the age of six years; and George, who is now a respectable merchant at Leghorn, in Tuscany.

All the offspring of my parents were, in their infancy, uncommonly handsome, excepting myself. The boys were fair and lusty, with auburn hair, light blue eyes, and countenances peculiarly animated and lovely. I was swarthy; my eyes were singularly large in proportion to my face, which was small and round, exhibiting features peculiarly marked with the most pensive and melancholy cast.

The great difference betwixt my brothers and myself, in point of personal beauty, tended much to endear me to my parents, particularly to my father, whom I strongly resembled. The early propensities of my life were tinctured with romantic and singular characteristics; some of which I shall here mention, as proofs that the mind is never to be diverted from its original bent, and that every event of my life has more or less been marked by the progressive evils of a too acute sensibility.

The nursery in which I passed my hours of infancy was so near the great aisle of the minster, that the organ, which re-echoed its deep tones, accompanied by the chaunting of the choristers, was distinctly heard both at morning and evening service. I remember with what pleasure I used to listen, and how much I was delighted whenever I was permitted to sit on the winding steps which led from the aisle to the cloisters. I can at this moment recall to memory the sensations I then experienced–the tones that seemed to thrill through my heart, the longing which I felt to unite my feeble voice to the full anthem, and the awful though sublime impression which the church service never failed to make upon my feelings. While my brothers were playing on the green before the minster, the servant who attended us has often, by my earnest entreaties, suffered me to remain beneath the great eagle which stood in the centre of the aisle, to support the book from which the clergyman read the lessons of the day; and nothing could keep me away, even in the coldest seasons, but the stern looks of an old man, whom I named Black John from the colour of his beard and complexion, and whose occupations within the sacred precincts were those of a bell-ringer and sexton.

As soon as I had learned to read my great delight was that of learning epitaphs and monumental inscriptions. A story of melancholy import never failed to excite my attention; and before I was seven years old I could correctly repeat Pope's Lines to the Memory of an Unfortunate Lady; Mason's Elegy on the Death of the beautiful Countess of Coventry, and many smaller poems on similar subjects. I had then been attended two years by various masters. Mr. Edmund Broadrip taught me music, my father having presented me with one of Kirkman's finest harpsichords, as an encitement to emulation. Even there my natural bent of mind evinced itself. The only melody which pleased me was that of the mournful and touching kind. Two of my earliest favourites were the celebrated ballad by Gay, beginning, "'Twas when the sea was roaring," and the simple pathetic stanzas of "The Heavy Hours," by the poet Lord Lyttelton. These, though nature had given me but little voice, I could at seven years of age sing so pathetically that my mother, to the latest hour of her life, never could bear to hear the latter of them repeated. They reminded her of sorrows in which I have since painfully learned to sympathise.

The early hours of boarding-school study I passed under the tuition of the Misses More, sisters to the lady of that name whose talents have been so often celebrated. [1] The education of their young pupils was undertaken by the five sisters. "In my mind's eye" I see them now before me; while every circumstance of those early days is minutely and indelibly impressed upon my memory.

I remember the first time I ever was present at a dramatic representation: it was the benefit of that great actor [1] who was proceeding rapidly towards the highest paths of fame, when death dropped the oblivious curtain, and closed the scene for ever. The part which he performed was King Lear; his wife, afterwards Mrs. Fisher, played Cordelia, but not with sufficient *éclat* to render the profession an object for her future exertions. The whole school attended; Mr. Powel's two daughters being then pupils of the Misses More. Mrs. John Kemble, then Miss P. Hopkins, was also one of my schoolfellows, as was the daughter of Mrs. Palmer, formerly Miss Pritchard, and afterwards Mrs. Lloyd. I mention these circumstances merely to prove that memory does not deceive me.

In my early days my father was prosperous, and my mother was the happiest of wives. She adored her children; she devoted her thoughts and divided her affections between them and the tenderest of husbands. Their spirits now, I trust, are in happier regions, blest, and reunited for ever.

If there could be found a fault in the conduct of my mother towards her children, it was that of a too unlimited indulgence, a too tender care, which but little served to arm their breast against the perpetual arrows of mortal vicissitude. My father's commercial concerns were crowned with prosperity. His house was opened by hospitality, and his generosity was only equalled by the liberality of fortune: every day augmented his successes; every hour seemed to increase his domestic felicity, till I attained my ninth year, when a change took place as sudden as it was unfortunate, at a moment when every luxury, every happiness, not only brightened the present, but gave promise of future felicity. A scheme was suggested to my father, as wild and romantic as it was perilous to hazard, which was no less than that of establishing a whale fishery on the coast of Labrador, and of civilising the Esquimaux Indians, in order to employ them in the extensive undertaking. During two years this eccentric plan occupied his thoughts by day, his dreams by night: all the smiles of prosperity could not tranquillise the restless spirit, and while he anticipated an acquirement of fame he little considered the perils that would attend his fortune.

My mother (who, content with affluence and happy in beholding the prosperity of her children, trembled at the fear of endangering either), in vain endeavoured to dissuade my father from putting his favourite scheme in practice. In the early part of his youth he had been accustomed to a sea life, and, being born an American, his restless spirit was ever busied in plans for the increase of wealth and honour to his native country, whose fame and interest were then united to those of Britain. After many dreams of success and many conflicts betwixt prudence and ambition, he resolved on putting his scheme in practice; the potent witchery possessed his brain, and all the persuasive powers of reason shrunk before its magic.

Full of the important business, my misguided parent repaired to the metropolis, and on his arrival laid the plan before the late Earl of Hilsborough, Sir Hugh Palliser, the late Earl of Bristol, Lord Chatham (father to the present Mr. William Pitt), the chancellor Lord Northington, who was my godfather, and several other equally distinguished personages; who all not only approved the plan but commended the laudable and public spirit which induced my father to suggest it. The prospect appeared full of promise, and the Labrador whale fishery was expected to be equally productive with that of Greenland. My parent's commercial connections were of the highest respectability, while his own name for worth and integrity gave a powerful sanction to the eccentric undertaking.

In order to facilitate this plan my father deemed it absolutely necessary to reside at least two years in America. My mother, who felt an invincible antipathy to the sea, heard his determination with grief and horror. All the persuasive powers of affection failed to detain him; all the pleadings of reason, prudence, a fond wife, and an infant family, proved ineffectual. My father was determined on departing, and my mother's unconquerable timidity prevented her being the companion of his voyage. From this epocha I date the sorrows of my family.

He sailed for America. His eldest son, John, was previously placed in a mercantile house at Leghorn. My younger brothers and myself remained with my mother at Bristol. Two years was the limited time of his absence, and, on his departure, the sorrow of my parents was reciprocal. My mother's heart was almost bursting with anguish; but even death would to her have been preferable to the horrors of crossing a tempestuous ocean and quitting her children, my father having resolved on leaving my brothers and myself in England for education.

Still the comforts, and even the luxuries of life distinguished our habitation. The tenderness of my mother's affection made her lavish of every elegance; and the darlings of her bosom were dressed, waited on, watched, and indulged with a degree of fondness bordering on folly. My clothes were sent for from London; my fancy was indulged to the extent of its caprices; I was flattered and praised into a belief that I was a being of superior order. To sing, to play a lesson on the harpsichord, to recite an elegy, and to make doggerel verses, made the extent of my occupations, while my person improved, and my mother's indulgence was almost unexampled.

My father, several years before his departure for America, had removed from the Minster House, and resided in one larger and more convenient for his increased family. This habitation was elegantly arranged; all the luxuries of plate, silk furniture, foreign wines, &c., evinced his knowledge of what was worth enjoying, and displayed that warm hospitality which is often the characteristic of a British merchant. This disposition for the good things of the world influenced even the disposal of his children's comforts. The bed in which I slept was of the richest crimson damask; the dresses which we wore were of the finest cambric; during the summer months we were sent to Clifton Hill for the advantages of a purer air; and I never was permitted to board at school, or to pass a night of separation from the fondest of mothers.

Many months elapsed, and my mother continued to receive the kindest letters from that husband whose rash scheme filled her bosom with regret and apprehension. At length the intervals became more frequent and protracted. The professions of regard, no longer flowing from the heart, assumed a laboured style, and seemed rather the efforts of honourable feeling than the involuntary language of confidential affection. My mother felt the change, and her affliction was infinite.

At length a total silence of several months awoke her mind to the sorrows of neglect, the torture of compunction; she now lamented the timidity which had divided her from a husband's bosom, the natural fondness which had bound her to her children; for while her heart bled with sorrow and palpitated with apprehension, the dreadful secret was unfolded, and the cause of my father's silence was discovered to be a new attachment–a mistress, whose resisting nerves could brave the stormy ocean, and who had consented to remain two years with him in the frozen wilds of America.

This intelligence nearly annihilated my mother, whose mind, though not strongly organised, was tenderly susceptible. She resigned herself to grief. I was then at an age to feel and to participate in her sorrows. I often wept to see her weep; I tried all my little skill to soothe her, but in vain: the first shock was followed by calamities of a different nature. The scheme in which my father had embarked his fortune failed, the Indians rose in a body, burnt his settlement, murdered many of his people, and turned the produce of their toil adrift on the wide and merciless ocean. The noble patrons of his plan deceived him in their assurances of marine protection, and the island of promise presented a scene of barbarous desolation. This misfortune was rapidly followed by other commercial losses; and to complete the vexations which pressed heavily on my mother, her rash husband gave a bill of sale of his whole property, by the authority of which we were obliged to quit our home, and to endure those accumulated vicissitudes for which there appeared no remedy.

It was at this period of trial that my mother was enabled to prove, by that unerring touchstone, adversity, who were her real and disinterested friends. Many, with affected commiseration, dropped a tear–or rather seemed to drop one–on the disappointments of our family; while others, with a malignant triumph, condemned the expensive style in which my father had reared his children, the studied elegance which had characterised my mother's dress and habitation, and the hospitality, which was now marked by the ungrateful epithet of prodigal luxuriance, but which had evinced the open liberality of my father's heart.

At this period my brother William died. He was only six years of age, but a promising and most lovely infant. His sudden death, in consequence of the measles, nearly deprived my mother of her senses. She was deeply affected; but she found, after a period of time, that consolation which, springing from the bosom of an amiable friend, doubly solaced her afflictions. This female was one of the most estimable of her sex; she had been the widow of Sir Charles Erskine, and was then the wife of a respectable medical man who resided at Bristol.

In the society of Lady Erskine my mother gradually recovered her serenity of mind, or rather found it soften into a religious resignation. But the event of her domestic loss by death was less painful than that which she felt in the alienation of my father's affections. She frequently heard that he resided in America with his mistress, till, at the expiration of another year, she received a summons to meet him in London.

Language would but feebly describe the varying emotions which struggled in her bosom. At this interesting era she was preparing to encounter the freezing scorn, or the contrite glances, of either an estranged or a repentant husband; in either case her situation was replete with anticipated chagrin, for she loved him too tenderly not to participate even in the anguish of his compunction. His letter, which was coldly civil, requested particularly that the children might be the companions of her journey. We departed for the metropolis.

I was not then quite ten years old, though so tall and formed in my person that I might have passed for twelve or thirteen. My brother

George was a few years younger. On our arrival in London we repaired to my fathers lodgings in Spring Gardens. He received us, after three years' absence, with a mixture of pain and pleasure; he embraced us with tears, and his voice was scarcely articulate. My mother's agitation was indescribable; she received a cold embrace at their meeting–it was the last she ever received from her alienated husband.

As soon as the first conflicts seemed to subside, my father informed my mother that he was determined to place my brother and myself at a school in the vicinity of London; that he purposed very shortly returning to America, and that he would readily pay for my mother's board in any private and respectable family. This information seemed like a death-blow to their domestic hopes. A freezing, formal, premeditated separation from a wife who was guiltless of any crime, who was as innocent as an angel, seemed the very extent of decided misery. It was in vain that my mother essayed to change his resolution, and influence his heart in pronouncing a milder judgment; my father was held by a fatal fascination; he was the slave of a young and artful woman, who had availed herself of his American solitude, to undermine his affections for his wife and the felicity of his family.

This deviation from domestic faith was the only dark shade that marked my father's character. He possessed a soul brave, liberal, enlightened and ingenuous. He felt the impropriety of his conduct. Yet, though his mind was strongly organised, though his understanding was capacious, and his sense of honour delicate even to fastidiousness, he was still the dupe of his passions, the victim of an unfortunate attachment.

Within a few days of our arrival in London we were placed for education in a school at Chelsea. The mistress of this seminary was perhaps one of the most extraordinary women that ever graced, or disgraced, society; her name was Meribah Lorrington. She was the most extensively accomplished female that I ever remember to have met with; her mental powers were no less capable of cultivation than superiorly cultivated. Her father, whose name was Hull, had from her infancy been the master of an academy at Earl's Court, near Fulham; and early after his marriage losing his wife, he resolved on giving this daughter a masculine education. Meribah was early instructed in all the modern accomplishments, as well as in classical knowledge. She was mistress of the Latin, French, and Italian languages; she was said to be a perfect arithmetician and astronomer, and possessed the art of painting on silk to a degree of exquisite perfection. But, alas! with all these advantages she was addicted to one vice, which at times so completely absorbed her faculties as to deprive her of every power, either mental or corporeal. Thus, daily and hourly, her superior acquirements, her enlightened understanding, yielded to the intemperance of her ruling infatuation, and every power of reflection seemed lost in the unfeminine propensity.

All that I ever learned I acquired from this extraordinary woman. In those hours when her senses were not intoxicated, she would delight in the task of instructing me. She had only five or six pupils, and it was my lot to be her particular favourite. She always, out of school, called me her little friend, and made no scruple of conversing with me (sometimes half the night, for I slept in her chamber), on domestic and confidential affairs. I felt for her a very sincere affection, and I listened with peculiar attention to all the lessons she inculcated. Once I recollect her mentioning the particular failing which disgraced so intelligent a being. She pleaded, in excuse of it, the immitigable regret of a widowed heart, and with compunction declared that she flew to intoxication as the only refuge from the pang of prevailing sorrow. I continued more than twelve months under the care of Mrs. Lorrington, during which period my mother boarded in a clergyman's family at Chelsea. I applied rigidly to study, and acquired a taste for books, which has never, from that time, deserted me. Mrs. Lorrington frequently read to me after school hours, and I to her. I sometimes indulged my fancy in writing verses, or composing rebuses, and my governess never failed to applaud the juvenile compositions I presented to her. Some of them, which I preserved and printed in a small volume shortly after my marriage, were written when I was between twelve and thirteen years of age; but as love was the theme of my poetical phantasies, I never showed them to my mother till I was about to publish them.

It was my custom, every Sunday evening, to drink tea with my mother. During one of those visits a captain in the British navy, a friend of my father's, became so partial to my person and manners that a proposal of marriage shortly after followed. My mother was astonished when she heard it, and, as soon as she recovered from her surprise, inquired of my suitor how old he thought me; his reply was, "About sixteen." My mother smiled, and informed him that I was then not quite thirteen. He appeared to be sceptical on the subject, till he was again assured of the fact, when he took his leave with evident chagrin, but not without expressing his hopes that, on his return to England–for he was going on a two years' expedition–I should be still disengaged. His ship foundered at sea a few months after, and this amiable gallant officer perished.

I had remained a year and two months with Mrs. Lorrington, when pecuniary derangements obliged her to give up her school. Her father's manners were singularly disgusting, as was his appearance; for he wore a silvery beard which reached to his breast; and a kind of Persian robe which gave him the external appearance of a necromancer. He was of the Anabaptist persuasion, and so stern in his conversation that the young pupils were exposed to perpetual terror. Added to these circumstances, the failing of his daughter became so evident, that even during school hours she was frequently in a state of confirmed intoxication. These events conspired to break up the establishment, and I was shortly after removed to a boarding-school at Battersea.

The mistress of this seminary, Mrs. Leigh, was a lively, sensible, and accomplished woman; her daughter was only a few years older than myself, and extremely amiable as well as lovely. Here I might have been happy, but my father's remissness in sending pecuniary supplies, and my mother's dread of pecuniary inconvenience, induced her to remove me; my brother, nevertheless, still remained under the care of the Reverend Mr. Gore, at Chelsea.

Several months elapsed, and no remittance arrived from my father. I was now near fourteen years old, and my mother began to foresee the vicissitudes to which my youth might be exposed, unprotected, tenderly educated, and without the advantages of fortune. My father's impracticable scheme had impoverished his fortune and deprived his children of that affluence which, in their infancy, they had been taught to hope for. I cannot speak of my own person, but my partial friends were too apt to flatter me. I was naturally of a pensive and melancholy character; my reflections on the changes of fortune frequently gave me an air of dejection which perhaps excited an interest beyond what might have been awakened by the vivacity or bloom of juvenility.

I adored my mother. She was the mildest, the most unoffending of existing mortals; her temper was cheerful, as her heart was innocent; she beheld her children as it seemed fatherless, and she resolved, by honourable means, to support them. For this purpose a convenient house was hired at Little Chelsea, and furnished, for a ladies' boarding-school. Assistants of every kind were engaged, and I was deemed worthy of an occupation that flattered my self-love and impressed my mind with a sort of domestic consequence. The English language was my department in the seminary, and I was permitted to select passages both in prose and verse for the studies of my infant pupils. It was also my occupation to superintend their wardrobes, to see them dressed and undressed by the servants or half-boarders, and to read sacred and moral lessons on saints' days and Sunday evenings.

Shortly after my mother had established herself at Chelsea, on a summer's evening, as I was sitting at the window, I heard a deep sigh, or rather a groan of anguish, which suddenly attracted my attention. The night was approaching rapidly, and I looked towards the gate before the house, where I observed a woman evidently labouring under excessive affliction; I instantly descended and approached her. She, bursting into tears, asked whether I did not know her. Her dress was torn and filthy; she was almost naked; and an old bonnet, which nearly hid her face, so completely disfigured her features that I had not the smallest idea of the person who was then almost sinking before me. I gave her a small sum of money, and inquired the cause of her apparent agony. She took my hand and pressed it to her lips. "Sweet girl, "said she, "you are still the angel I ever knew you!" I was astonished. She raised her bonnet–her fine dark eyes met mine. It was Mrs. Lorrington. I led her into the house; my mother was not at home. I took her to my chamber, and, with the assistance of a lady who was our French teacher, I clothed and comforted her. She refused to say how she came to be in so deplorable a situation, and took her leave. It was in vain that I entreated, that I conjured her to let me know where I might send to her. She refused to give me her address, but promised that in a few days she would call on me again. It is impossible to describe the wretched appearance of this accomplished woman! The failing to which she had now yielded, as to a monster that would destroy her, was evident even at the moment when she was speaking to me. I saw no more of her; but to my infinite regret I was informed some years after that she had died, the martyr of a premature decay, brought on by the indulgence of her propensity to intoxication, in the workhouse of Chelsea!

The number of my mother's pupils in a few months amounted to ten or twelve, and just at a period when an honourable independence promised to cheer the days of an unexampled parent, my father unexpectedly returned from America. The pride of his soul was deeply wounded by the step which my mother had taken; he was offended even beyond the bounds of reason: he considered his name as disgraced, his conjugal reputation tarnished, by the public mode which his wife had adopted of revealing to the world her unprotected situation. A prouder heart never palpitated in the breast of man than that of my father: tenacious of fame, ardent in the pursuit of visionary schemes, he could not endure the exposure of his altered fortune; while Hope still beguiled him with her flattering promise that time would favour his projects, and fortune, at some future period, reward him with success.

At the expiration of eight months my mother, by my father's positive command, broke up her establishment and returned to London. She engaged lodgings in the neighbourhood of Marylebone. My father then resided in Green Street, Grosvenor Square. His provision for his family was scanty, his visits few. He had a new scheme on foot respecting the Labrador coast, the particulars of which I do not remember, and all his zeal, united with all his interest, was employed in promoting its accomplishment. My mother, knowing that my father publicly resided with his mistress, did not even hope for his returning affection. She devoted herself to her children, and endured her sorrows with the patience of conscious rectitude.

At this period my father frequently called upon us, and often attended me while we walked in the fields near Marylebone. His conversation was generally of a domestic nature, and he always lamented that fatal attachment which was now too strongly cemented by time and obligations ever to be dissolved without an ample provision for Elenor, which was the name of my father's mistress. In one of our morning walks we called upon the Earl of Northington, my father having some commercial business to communicate to his lordship. Lord Northington then resided in Berkeley Square, two doors from Hill Street, in the house which is now occupied by Lord Robert Spencer. We were received with the most marked attention and politeness (I was presented as the god-daughter of the late Chancellor Lord Northington), and my father was requested to dine with his lordship a few days after. From this period I frequently saw Lord Northington, and always experienced from him the most flattering and gratifying civility. I was then a child, not more than fourteen years of age.

The finishing points of my education I received at Oxford House, Marylebone. I was at this period within a few months of fifteen years of age, tall, and nearly such as my partial friends, the few whose affection has followed me from childhood, remember me. My early love for lyric harmony had led me to a fondness for the more sublime scenes of dramatic poetry. I embraced every leisure moment to write verses; I even fancied that I could compose a tragedy, and more than once unsuccessfully attempted the arduous undertaking.

The dancing-master at Oxford House, Mr. Hussey, was then ballet-master at Covent Garden Theatre. Mrs. Hervey, the governess, mentioned me to him as possessing an extraordinary genius for dramatic exhibitions. My figure was commanding for my age, and (my father's pecuniary embarrassments augmenting by the failure of another American project) my mother was consulted as to the propriety of my making the stage my profession. Many cited examples of females who, even in that perilous and arduous situation, preserved an unspotted fame, inclined her to listen to the suggestion, and to allow of my consulting some master of the art as to my capability of becoming an ornament to the theatre.

Previous to this idea my father had again quitted England. He left his wife with assurances of good-will–his children with all the agonies of parental regret. When he took leave of my mother, his emphatic words were these–I never shall forget them–"Take care that no dishonour falls upon my daughter. If she is not safe at my return I will annihilate you! "My mother heard the stern injunction, and trembled while he repeated it.

I was, in consequence of my wish to appear on the stage, introduced to Mr. Hull [1] of Covent Garden Theatre; he then resided in King Street, Soho. He heard me recite some passages of the character of Jane Shore, and seemed delighted with my attempt. I was shortly after presented, by a friend of my mother's, to Mr. Garrick [2]; Mr. Murphy, [3] the celebrated dramatic poet, was one of the party, and we passed the evening at the house of the British Roscius in the Adelphi. This was during the last year that he dignified the profession by his public appearance. Mr. Garrick's encomiums were of the most gratifying kind. He determined that he would appear in the same play with me on the first night's trial; but what part to choose for my *début* was a difficult question. I was too young for anything beyond the girlish character; and the dignity of tragedy afforded but few opportunities for the display of such juvenile talents. After some hesitation my tutor fixed on the part of Cordelia. His own Lear can never be forgotten.

It was not till the period when everything was arranged for my appearance that the last solemn injunction, so emphatically uttered by my father, nearly palsied my mother's resolution. She dreaded the perils, the temptations to which an unprotected girl would be exposed in so public a situation; while my ardent fancy was busied in contemplating a thousand triumphs, in which my vanity would be publicly gratified without the smallest sacrifice of my private character.

While this plan was in agitation, I was one evening at Drury Lane Theatre with my mother and a small party of her friends, when an officer entered the box. His eyes were fixed on me, and his persevering attention at length nearly overwhelmed me with confusion. The entertainment being finished, we departed. The stranger followed us. At that period my mother resided in Southampton Buildings, Chancery Lane, for the protection which a venerable and respectable friend offered at a moment when it was so necessary. This friend was the late Samuel Cox, Esq., the intimate friend of Mr. Garrick, and an honour to those laws of which he was a distinguished professor.

It was Mr. Garrick's particular request that I would frequent the theatre as much as possible till the period fixed on for my appearance on the stage. I had now just completed my fifteenth year, and my little heart throbbed with impatience for the hour of trial. My tutor was most sanguine in his expectations of my success, and every rehearsal seemed to strengthen his flattering opinion.

It happened that, several evenings following, the stranger officer, whose name, for motives of delicacy towards his family, I forbear to mention, followed me to and from the theatre. It was in vain that he offered his attentions in the box; my mother's frown and assiduous care repulsed them effectually. But the perseverance of a bad mind in the accomplishment of a bad action is not to be subdued. A letter was written and conveyed to me through the hands of a female servant; I opened it; I read a declaration of the most ardent love. The writer avowed himself the son of Lady —, and offered marriage; he was graceful and handsome. I instantly delivered the letter to my mother, and shortly after he was, by an acquaintance, presented with decorous ceremony.

The idea of my appearing on the stage seemed to distract this accomplished suitor. My mother, who but *half* approved a dramatic life, was more than *half* inclined to favour the addresses of Captain —. The injunction of my father every hour became more indelibly impressed on her memory; she knew his stern and invincible sense of honour too well to hazard the thought of awakening it to vengeance.

After a short period the friend who had presented Captain—, alarmed for my safety, and actuated by a liberal wish to defend me from the artifice of his associate, waited on my mother, and, after some hesitation, informed her that my lover was already married! that he had a young and amiable wife in a sister kingdom, and that he apprehended some diabolical stratagem for the enthralment of my honour. My mother's consternation was infinite. The important secret was communicated to me, and I felt little regret in the loss of a husband when I reflected that a matrimonial alliance would have compelled me to relinquish my theatrical profession.

I had also at this period another professed admirer; a man of a splendid fortune, but nearly old enough to be my grandfather. This suit I never would listen to; and the drama, the delightful drama, seemed the very criterion of all human happiness.

I now found myself an object of attention whenever I appeared at the theatre. I had been too often in public not to be observed, and it was buzzed about that I was the juvenile pupil of Garrick–the promised Cordelia. My person improved daily; yet a sort of dignified air, which from a child I had acquired, effectually shielded me from the attacks of impertinence or curiosity. Garrick was delighted with everything I did. He would sometimes dance a minuet with me, sometimes request me to sing the favourite ballads of the day; but the circumstance which most pleased him was my tone of voice, which he frequently told me closely resembled that of his favourite Cibber. [1]

Never shall I forget the enchanting hours which I passed in Mr. Garrick's society; he appeared to me as one who possessed more power, both to awe and to attract, than any man I ever met with. His smile was fascinating, but he had at times a restless peevishness of tone which excessively affected his hearers; at least it affected me so that I never shall forget it.

Opposite to the house in which I resided lived John Vernon, Esq., an eminent solicitor. I observed a young inmate of his habitation frequently watching me with more than ordinary attention. He was handsome in person, and his countenance was overcast by a sort of languor, the effect of sickness, which rendered it peculiarly interesting. Frequently when I approached the window of our drawing-room this young observer would bow or turn away with evident emotion. I related the circumstance to my mother, and from that time the lower shutters of our windows were perpetually closed. The young lawyer often excited my mirth, and my mother's indignation; and the injunction of my father was frequently repeated by her, with the addition of her wish, that I was "once well married."

Every attention which was now paid to me augmented my dear mother's apprehensions. She fancied every man a seducer, and every hour an hour of accumulating peril! I know what she was doomed to feel, for that Being who formed my sensitive and perpetually aching heart knows that I have *since felt it.*

Among other friends who were in the habit of visiting my mother there was one, a Mr. Wayman, an attorney, of whom she entertained the highest opinion. He was distinguished by the patronage of Mr. Cox, and his reputation required no other voucher. One evening a party of six was proposed for the following Sunday; with much persuasion my mother consented to go, and to allow that I should also attend her. Greenwich was the place fixed on for the dinner, and we prepared for the day of recreation. It was then the fashion to wear silks. I remember that I wore a nightgown of pale blue lustring, with a chip hat trimmed with ribands of the same colour. Never was I dressed so perfectly to my own satisfaction; I anticipated a day of admiration. Heaven can bear witness that to me it was a day of fatal victory!

On our stopping at the "Star and Garter," at Greenwich, the person who came to hand me from the carriage was our opposite neighbour in Southampton Buildings. I was confused; but my mother was indignant. Mr. Wayman presented his young friend–that friend who was ordained to be MY HUSBAND!

Our party dined, and early in the evening we returned to London. Mr. Robinson remained at Greenwich for the benefit of the air, being recently recovered from a fit of sickness. During the remainder of the evening Mr. Wayman expatiated on the many good qualities of his friend Mr. Robinson: spoke of his future expectations from a rich old uncle; of his probable advancement in his profession; and, more than all, of his enthusiastic admiration of me.

A few days after Mr. Robinson paid my mother a visit. We had now removed to Villars Street, York Buildings. My mother's fondness for books of a moral and religious character was not lost upon my new lover, and elegantly bound editions of Hervey's "Meditations," with some others of a similar description, were presented as small tokens of admiration and respect. My mother was beguiled by these little interesting attentions, and soon began to feel a strong predilection in favour of Mr. Robinson.

Every day some new mark of respect augmented my mother's favourable opinion; till Mr. Robinson became so great a favourite that he seemed to her the most perfect of existing beings. Just at this period my brother George sickened for the smallpox; my mother idolised him; he was dangerously ill. Mr. Robinson was indefatigable in his attentions, and my appearance on the stage was postponed till the period of his perfect recovery. Day and night Mr. Robinson devoted himself to the task of consoling my mother, and of attending to her darling boy; hourly, and indeed momentarily, Mr. Robinson's praises were reiterated with enthusiasm by my mother. He was "the kindest, the best of mortals! "The least addicted to worldly follies, and the man, of all others, whom she should adore as a *son-in law*.

My brother recovered at the period when I sickened from the infection of his disease. I felt little terror at the approaches of a dangerous and deforming malady; for, I know not why, but personal beauty has never been to me an object of material solicitude. It was now that Mr. Robinson exerted all his assiduity to win my affections; it was when a destructive disorder menaced my features, and the few graces that nature had lent them, that he professed a disinterested fondness; every day he attended with the zeal of a brother, and that zeal made an impression of gratitude upon my heart, which was the source of all my succeeding sorrows.

During my illness Mr. Robinson so powerfully wrought upon the feelings of my mother, that she prevailed on me to promise, in case I should recover, to give him my hand in marriage. The words of my father were frequently repeated, not without some innuendoes that I refused my ready consent to a union with Mr. Robinson, from a blind partiality to the libertine Captain—. Repeatedly urged and hourly reminded of my father's vow, I at last consented, and the banns were published while I was yet lying on a bed of sickness. I was then only a few months advanced in my sixteenth year.

My mother, whose affection for me was boundless, notwithstanding her hopes of my forming an alliance that would be productive of felicity, still felt the most severe pain at the thought of our approaching separation. She was estranged from a husband's affections; she had treasured up all her fondest hopes in the society of an only daughter; she knew that no earthly pleasure can compensate for the loss of that sweet sympathy which is the bond of union betwixt child and parent. Her regrets were infinite as they were evident, and Mr. Robinson, in order to remove any obstacle which this consideration might throw in the way of our marriage, voluntarily proposed that she should reside with us. He represented me as too young and inexperienced to superintend domestic concerns; and while he flattered my mother's *amour propre* he rather requested her aid as a sacrifice to his interest than as an obligation conferred on her.

The banns were published three successive Sundays at St. Martin's Church, and the day was fixed for our marriage– *the twelfth of April*. It was not till all preliminaries were adjusted that Mr. Robinson, With much apparent agitation, suggested the necessity of keeping our union a secret. I was astonished at the proposal; but two reasons were given for his having made it, both of which seemed plausible; the first was, that Mr. Robinson had still three months to serve before his articles to Messrs. Vernon and Elderton expired; and the second was, the hope which a young lady entertained of forming a matrimonial union with Mr. Robinson as soon as that period should arrive. The latter reason alarmed me, but I was most solemnly assured that all the affection was cherished on the lady's part–that Mr. Robinson was particularly averse to the idea of such a marriage, and that as soon as he should become of age his independence would place him beyond the control of any person whatsoever.

I now proposed deferring our wedding-day till that period. I pleaded that I thought myself too young to encounter the cares and important duties of domestic life; I shrunk from the idea of everything clandestine, and anticipated a thousand ill consequences that might attend on a concealed marriage. My scruples only seemed to increase Mr. Robinson's impatience for that ceremony which should make me his for ever. He represented to my mother the disapprobation which my father would not fail to evince at my adopting a theatrical life in preference to engaging in an honourable and prosperous connection. He so powerfully worked upon the credulity of my beloved parent that she became a decided convert to his opinions. My youth, my person, he represented as the destined snares for my honour on a public stage, where all the attractions of the mimic scene would combine to render me a fascinating object. He also persuaded her that my health would suffer by the fatigues and exertions of the profession, and that probably I might be induced to marry some man who would not approve of a *mother's forming* a part in our *domestic establishments*.

These circumstances were repeatedly urged in favour of the union. Still I felt an almost instinctive repugnance at the thought of a clandestine marriage. My mother, whose parental fondness was ever watchful for my safety, now imagined that my objections proceeded from a fixed partiality towards the libertine Captain—, who, though he had not the temerity to present himself before my mother, persisted in writing to me, and in following me whenever I appeared in public. I never spoke to him after the story of his marriage was repeated to my mother; I never corresponded with him, but felt a decided and proud indignation whenever his name was mentioned in my presence.

My appearance on the stage had been put off from time to time, till Mr. Garrick became impatient, and desired my mother to allow of his fixing the night of important trial. It was now that Mr. Robinson and my mother united in persuading me to relinquish my project; and so perpetually, during three days, was I tormented on the subject—so ridiculed for having permitted the banns to be published, and afterwards hesitating to fulfil my contract, that I consented—and was married.

As soon as the day of my wedding was fixed, it was deemed necessary that a total revolution should take place in my external appearance. I had till that period worn the habit of a child, and the dress of a woman so suddenly assumed sat rather awkwardly upon me. Still, so juvenile was my appearance, that even two years after my union with Mr. Robinson I was always accosted with the appellation of *Miss* whenever I entered a shop or was in company with strangers. My manners were no less childish than my appearance; only three months before I became a wife I had dressed a doll, and such was my dislike to the idea of a matrimonial alliance that the only circumstance which induced me to marry was that of being still permitted to reside with my mother, and to live separated, at least for some time, from my husband.

My heart, even when I knelt at the altar, was as free from any tender impression as it had been at the moment of my birth. I knew not the sensation of any sentiment beyond that of esteem; love was still a stranger to my bosom. I had never, then, seen the being who was destined to inspire a thought which might influence my fancy or excite an interest in my mind, and I well remember that even while I was pronouncing the marriage vow my fancy involuntarily wandered to that scene where I had hoped to support myself with *èclat* and reputation.

The ceremony was performed by Dr. Saunders, the venerable vicar of St. Martin's, who, at the conclusion of the ceremony, declared that he had never before performed the office for so young a bride. The clerk officiated as father; my mother and the woman who opened the pews were the only witnesses to the union. I was dressed in the habit of a Quaker–a society to which, in early youth, I was particularly partial. From the church we repaired to the house of a female friend, where a splendid breakfast was waiting; I changed my dress to one of white muslin, a chip hat adorned with white ribbons, a white sarsnet scarf-cloak, and slippers of white satin embroidered with silver. I mention these trifling circumstances because they lead to some others of more importance.

From the house of my mother's friend we set out for the inn at Maidenhead Bridge, Mr. Robinson and myself in a phaeton, my mother in a post-chaise; we were also accompanied by a gentleman by the name of Balack, a very intimate acquaintance and schoolfellow of my husband, who was not apprised of our wedding, but who nevertheless considered Mr. Robinson as my avowed suitor.

On his first seeing me, he remarked that I was *"dressed like a bride"*. The observation overwhelmed me with confusion. During the day I was more than pensive–I was melancholy; I considered all that had passed as a vision, and would scarcely persuade myself that the union which I had permitted to be solemnised was indissoluble. My mother frequently remarked my evident chagrin; and in the evening, while we strolled together in the garden which was opposite the inn, I told her, with a torrent of tears, the vouchers of my sincerity, that I was the most wretched of mortals! That I felt the most perfect esteem for Mr. Robinson, but that, according to my ideas of domestic happiness, there should be a warm and powerful union of soul, to which I was yet totally a stranger.

Mrs Robinson

During my absence from town a letter was written to Mr. Garrick, informing him that an advantageous marriage (for my mother considered Mr. Robinson as the legal heir to a handsome fortune, together with an estate in South Wales) had induced me to relinquish my theatrical prospects; and a few weeks after, meeting Mr. Garrick in the street, he congratulated me on my union, and expressed the warmest wishes for my future happiness.

The day after our marriage Mr. Robinson proposed dining at Henley-upon-Thames. My mother would not venture in the phaeton, and Mr. Balack occupied the place which was declined by her. On taking his seat between Robinson and myself, he remarked, "Were you *married* I should think of the holy anathema–Cursed is he that parteth *man* and *wife* "My countenance was suddenly suffused with the deepest scarlet; I cautiously concealed the effect which his remarks had produced, and we proceeded on our journey.

Descending a steep hill betwixt Maidenhead Thicket and Henley, we met a drove of oxen. The comic opera of the Padlock was then in high celebrity, and our facetious little friend a second time disconcerted me by saying, in the words of Don Diego, "I don't like oxen, I wish they had been a flock of sheep!" I now began to discover the variety of unpleasant sensations which, even undesignedly, must arise from conversation, in the presence of those who were clandestinely married. I also trembled with apprehension, lest anything disgraceful should attach itself to my fame, by being seen under doubtful circumstances in the society of Mr. Robinson .

On our return to London, after ten days'absence, a house was hired in Great Queen Street, Lincoln's Inn Fields. It was a large old-fashioned mansion, and stood on the spot where the Freemasons'Tavern has been since erected. This house was the property of a lady, an acquaintance of my mother, the widow of Mr. Worlidge, an artist of considerable celebrity. It was handsomely furnished, and contained many valuable pictures by various masters. I resided with my mother; Mr. Robinson continued at the house of Messrs. Vernon and Elderton, in Southampton Buildings.

The stated time of concealment elapsed, and still my husband was perpetually at chambers in Lincoln's Inn. Still he was evidently under the control of his articles, and still desirous that our marriage should be kept a secret. My mother began to feel a considerable degree of inquietude upon the subject; particularly as she was informed that Mr. Robinson was not exactly in that state of expectation which he had represented. She found that he was already of age, and that he had still some months to serve of his clerkship. She also heard that he was not the nephew and heir, but the illegitimate son of the man from whom he expected a handsome fortune; though he had an elder brother, now Commodore William Robinson, who was then in India, reaping the fruits of industry under the patronage of Lord Clive.

It was now for the first time that my mother repented the influence she had used in promoting our union. She informed Mr. Robinson that she apprehended some gross deception on his part, and that she would no longer consent to our marriage being kept a secret. The reputation of a darling child, she alleged, was at stake; and though during a few weeks the world might have been kept in ignorance of my marriage, some circumstances that had transpired, now rendered an immediate disclosure absolutely necessary.

Mr. Robinson, finding my mother inexorable, resolved on setting out for Wales, in order to avow our marriage, and to present me to his *uncle* for such he still obstinately denominated his father. My mother wished to avail herself of this opportunity to visit her friends at Bristol, and accordingly we set out on the journey. We passed through Oxford; visited the different colleges; proceeded to Blenheim, and made the *tour* a tour of pleasure, with the hope of soothing my mother's resentment, and exhilarating my spirits, which were now perpetually dejected. I cannot help mentioning that, shortly after my marriage, I formed an acquaintance with a young lady, whose mind was no less romantic than my own, and while Mr. Robinson was occupied at chambers we almost daily passed our morning hours in Westminster Abbey. It was to me a soothing and a gratifying scene of meditation. I have often remained in the gloomy chapels of that sublime fabric till I became as it were an inhabitant of another world. The dim light of the Gothic windows, the vibration of my footsteps along the lofty aisles, the train of reflections that the scene inspired, were all suited to the temper of my soul; and the melancholy propensities of my earliest infancy seemed to revive with an instinctive energy, which rendered them the leading characteristics of my existence. Indeed the world has mistaken the character of my mind; I have ever been the reverse of volatile and dissipated. I mean not to write my own eulogy, though with the candid and sensitive mind I shall, I trust, succeed in my vindication

On our arrival at Bristol Mr. Robinson thought it most advisable to proceed towards Tregunter, the seat of his *uncle* alone, in order to prepare him for my cordial reception, or to avoid the mortification I should experience, should he refuse to sanction our union. Mr. Robinson left me a few guineas, and promised that his absence should be short and his affection increasing.

I had now been married near four months; and, though love was not the basis of my fidelity, honour, and a refined sense of feminine rectitude, attached me to the interest as well as to the person of my husband. I considered chastity as the brightest ornament that could embellish the female mind, and I regulated my conduct to that tenor which has principle more than affection to strengthen its progress.

At Bristol my mother experienced the most gratifying reception; all her former friends rejoiced to see her; I was invited daily to feasts of hospitality, and I found that fortune was to common minds a never-failing passport. Mr. Robinson was represented as a young man of considerable expectations, and his wife was consequently again received as the daughter of Mr. Darby. The house in which I first opened my eyes to this world of sorrow, the minster, its green, the school-house where I had passed many days, the tomb of my lost relatives in the church of St. Augustine were all visited by me with a sweet and melancholy interest. But the cathedral, the brass eagle in the middle aisle, under which, when an infant, I used to sit and join in the loud anthem, or chant the morning service, most sensibly attached me. I longed again to occupy my place beneath its expanding wings, and once I went before the service began to gratify my inclination.

Language cannot describe the sort of sensation which I felt when I heard the well-known, long-remembered organ flinging its loud peal through the Gothic structure. I hastened to the cloisters. The nursery windows were dim and shattered; the house was sinking to decay. The mouldering walk was gloomy, and my spirits were depressed beyond description: I stood alone, rapt in meditation. "Here," said I, "did my infant feet pace to and fro; here did I climb the long stone bench, and swiftly measure it at the peril of my safety. On those dark and winding steps did I sit and listen to the full-toned organ, the loud anthem, and the bell which called the parishioners to prayer. "I entered the cathedral once more; I read and re-read the monumental inscriptions; I paused upon the grave of Powell; I dropped a tear on the small square ground tablet which bore the name of Evelyn. Ah! How little has the misjudging world known of what has passed in my mind, even in the apparently gayest moments of my existence!

How much have I regretted that ever I was born, even when I have been surrounded with all that could gratify the vanity of woman!

Mr. Robinson on his arrival at Tregunter despatched a letter informing me that his *uncle* seemed disposed to act handsomely, but that he had only ventured to avow an intention to marry, fearful of abruptly declaring that he had been already some months a husband. Mr. Harris, for that was the name of my father-in-law, replied that "he hoped the object of his choice was not *too young* "At this question Mr. Robinson was somewhat disconcerted. "A young wife, "continued Mr. Harris, "cannot mend a man's fortune. How old is the girl you have chosen? "

"She is nearly seventeen! "

I was then only fifteen and a few months. [1]

"I hope she is not handsome, "was the second observation. "You say she is not rich; and beauty without money is but a dangerous sort of portion."

"Will you see her?"

"I have no objection," said Mr. Harris.

"She is now with her mother at Bristol—for," continued Mr. Robinson, with some hesitation, *"she is my wife"*

Mr. Harris paused, and then replied, "Well! Stay with me only a few days, and then you shall fetch her. If the thing is done, it cannot be undone. She is a gentlewoman you say, and I can have no reason to refuse seeing her."

The same letter which contained this intelligence also requested me to prepare for my journey, and desired me to write to a person whom Mr. Robinson named in London, and whom I had seen in his company, for a sum of money which would be necessary for our journey. This person was Mr. John King, then a money-broker in

Goodman's Fields; but I was an entire stranger to the transaction which rendered him the temporary source of my husband's finances.

One or two letters passed on this subject, and I waited anxiously for my presentation at Tregunter. At length the period of Mr. Robinson's return arrived and we set out together, while my mother remained with her friends at Bristol. Crossing the old passage to Chepstow in an open boat, a distance, though not extended, extremely perilous, we found the tide so strong and the night so boisterous that we were apprehensive of much danger. The rain poured and the wind blew tempestuously. The boat was full of passengers, and at one end of it were placed a drove of oxen. My terror was infinite; I considered this storm as an ill omen, but little thought that at future periods of my life I should have cause to regret that *I had nor perished!*

During our journey Robinson entreated me to overlook anything harsh that might appear in the manners of his *uncle* –for he still denied that Mr. Harris was his father. But above all things he conjured me to conceal my real age, and to say that I was some years older than he knew me to be. To this proposal I readily consented, and I felt myself firm in courage at the moment when we came within sight of Tregunter.

Mr. Harris was then building the family mansion, and resided in a pretty little decorated cottage which was afterwards converted into domestic offices. We passed through a thick wood, the mountains at every break meeting our eyes covered with thin clouds, and rising in a sublime altitude above the valley. A more romantic space of scenery never met the human eye! I felt my mind inspired with a pensive melancholy, and was only awakened from my reverie by the postboy stopping at the mansion of Tregunter.

Mr. Harris came out to receive me. I wore a dark claret-coloured riding habit, with a white beaver hat and feathers. He embraced me with excessive cordiality, while Miss Robinson, my husband's sister, with cold formality led me into the house. I never shall forget her looks or her manner. Had her brother presented the most abject being to her, she could not have taken my hand with a more frigid

31

demeanour. Miss Robinson, though not more than twenty years of age, was Gothic in her appearance and stiff in her deportment; she was of low stature and clumsy, with a countenance peculiarly formed for the expression of sarcastic vulgarity–a short snub nose, turned up at the point, a head thrown back with an air of *hauteur* ; a gaudy-coloured chintz gown, a thrice-bordered cap, with a profusion of ribbons, and a countenance somewhat more ruddy than was consistent with even pure health, presented the personage whom I was to know as my future companion and kinswoman!

Mr. Harris looked like a venerable *Hawthorn* a brown fustian coat, a scarlet waistcoat edged with narrow gold, a pair of woollen spatter-dashes, and a gold-laced hat, formed the dress he generally wore. He always rode a small Welsh pony, and was seldom in the house except at eating-time from sunrise to the close of the evening.

There was yet another personage in the domestic establishment, who was by Mr. Harris regarded as of no small importance: this was a venerable housekeeper of the name of Mary Edwards. Mrs. Molly was the female Mentor of the family; she dined at the table with Mr. Harris; she was the governess of the domestic department; and a more overbearing, vindictive spirit never inhabited the heart of mortal than that which pervaded the soul of the ill-natured Mrs. Molly.

It may easily be conjectured that my time passed heavily in this uninteresting circle. I was condemned either to drink ale with "the squire," for Mr. Harris was only spoken of by that title, or to visit the Methodistical seminary which Lady Huntingdon had established at Trevecca, another mansion house on the estate of Mr. Harris. Miss Robinson was of this sect; and though Mr. Harris was not a disciple of the Huntingdonian School, he was a constant church visitor on every Sunday. His zeal was indefatigable; and he would frequently fine the rustics (for he was a justice of the peace, and had been sheriff of the county) when he heard them swear, though every third sentence he uttered was attended by an oath that made his hearers shudder.

I soon became a considerable favourite of "the squire," but I did not find any yielding qualities about the hearts of Miss Betsy or Mrs. Molly. They observed me with jealous eyes; they considered me as an interloper, whose manners attracted Mr. Harris's esteem, and who was likely to diminish their divided influence in the family. I found them daily growing weary of my society; I perceived their side-long glances when I was complimented by the visiting neighbours on my good looks or taste in the choice of my dresses. Miss Robinson rode on horseback in a camlet safeguard, with a high-crowned bonnet; I wore a fashionable habit, and looked like something human. Envy at length assumed the form of insolence, and I was taunted perpetually on the folly of appearing like a woman of fortune; that a lawyer's wife had no right to dress like a duchess; and that, though I might be very accomplished, a good housewife had no occasion for harpsichords and books–they belonged to women who brought wherewithal to support them. Such was the language of vulgar, illiberal natures! Yet for three weeks I endured it patiently.

Knowing that Mr. Harris was disposed to think favourably of me– that he even declared he should "have liked me for his wife, had I not *"married Tom"* though he was then between sixty and seventy years of age, I thought it most prudent to depart, lest through the machinations of Miss Betsy and Mrs. Molly I should lose the share I had gained in his affections. My mother was still at Bristol; and the morning of our departure being arrived, to my infinite astonishment Mr. Harris proposed accompanying us thither. It was in vain that Molly and Miss interfered to prevent him; he swore that he would see me safe across the channel, whatever might be the consequence of his journey. We set out together.

On our arrival at Bristol Mr. Harris was presented to my mother, and by her introduced to many respectable friends. He was consequently invited to several dinner parties. I was his idol; he would dance with me; when he had taken the evening draught he would sing with me, and I was to him the most delightful of beings. Many embellishments for Tregunter House were submitted to my taste and choice; and I remember, on his giving orders for the marble chimney-pieces, he said, "Choose them as you like them, Mrs. Robinson, for they are all for you and Tom when I am no more." Indeed he frequently assured me, while I was at Tregunter, that the estate should be my husband's.

After passing many days at Bristol Mr. Harris returned to Wales, and our party set out for London. Mr. Robinson's mind was easy, and his hopes were confirmed by the kindness of his uncle; he now considered himself as the most happy of mortals. We removed from Great Queen Street to a house, No. I3, in Hatton Garden, which had been recently built. Mr. Robinson hired it, and furnished it with peculiar elegance. I frequently inquired into the extent of his finances, and he as often assured me that they were in every respect competent to his expenses. In addition to our domestic establishment Mr. Robinson purchased a handsome phaeton, with saddle horses for his own use; and I now made my *début* though scarcely emerged beyond the boundaries of childhood, in the broad hemisphere of fashionable folly.

A new face, a young person dressed with peculiar but simple elegance, was sure to attract attention at places of public entertainment. The first time I went to Ranelagh my habit was so singularly plain and Quaker-like that all eyes were fixed upon me. I wore a gown of light brown lustring with close round cuffs (it was then the fashion to wear long ruffles); my hair was without powder, and my head adorned with a plain round cap and a white chip hat, without any ornaments whatever.

The second place of polite entertainment to which Mr. Robinson accompanied me was the Pantheon concert, then the most fashionable assemblage of the gay and the distinguished. At this place it was customary to appear much dressed; large hoops and high feathers were universally worn. My habit was composed of pale pink satin, trimmed with broad sable; my dear mother presented me a suit of rich and valuable point lace, which she had received from my father as a birthday gift, and I was at least some hours employed in decorating my person for this new sphere of fascination: I say some hours, because my shape at that period required some arrangement, owing to the visible increase of my domestic solicitudes.

As soon as I entered the Pantheon rotunda, I never shall forget the impression which my mind received: the splendour of the scene, the dome illuminated with variegated lamps, the music, and the beauty of the women, seemed to present a circle of enchantment. I recollect that the most lovely of fair forms met my eyes in that of Lady Almeria Carpenter. The countenance which most pleased me was that of the late Mrs. Baddeley. [1] The first Countess of Tyrconnel also appeared with considerable *éclat*. But the buzz of the room, the unceasing murmur of admiration, attended the Marchioness Townshend. I took my seat on a sofa nearly opposite to that on which she was sitting, and I observed two persons, evidently men of fashion speaking to her, till one of them, looking towards me, with an audible voice inquired of the other, "Who is she?"

Their fixed stare disconcerted me; I rose, and, leaning on my husband's arm, again mingled in the brilliant circle. The inquiries followed us; stopping several friends, as we walked round the circle, and repeatedly demanding of them, "Who is that young lady in the pink dress trimmed with sable?" My manner and confusion plainly evinced that I was not accustomed to the gaze of impertinent high breeding. I felt uneasy, and proposed returning home, when I perceived that our two followers were joined by a third, who, on looking at me, said, "I think I know her." It was the late Earl of Northington. [1]

We had now to pass the group in order to quit the rotunda. Lord Northington, leaving his companions, approached me. "Miss Darby, or I am mistaken," said he, with a bow of marked civility. I replied that my name was now changed to that of Robinson, and, to prevent any awkward embarrassment, presented my husband, on whose arm I was still leaning. Lord Northington continued to walk round the Pantheon with us, made many inquiries after my father, complimented me on the improvement of my person, and "hoped that he should be permitted to pay his respects to Mr. and Mrs. Robinson."

We now entered the tea-room; there was not a seat vacant; I was considerably fatigued, and somewhat faint with the heat of the rotunda. I quitted the tea-room, and seated myself on a sofa near the door. In a few minutes Lord Northington brought me a cup of tea, for Mr. Robinson did not like to leave me alone, and at the same time presented his two inquisitive friends, Lord Lyttelton and Captain Ayscough. [1]

I now proposed departing. Mr. Robinson accompanied me to the vestibule, and while he was seeking the carriage Lord Lyttelton offered his services. I had never till that evening heard his name, but there was an easy effrontery in his address that completely disgusted, while his determined gaze distressed and embarrassed me, and I felt inexpressible satisfaction when Mr. Robinson returned to tell me that the carriage was ready.

On the following morning Lords Northington, Lyttelton, and Colonel Ayscough made their visits of ceremony. Mr. Robinson was not at home, but I received them, though not without some embarrassment. I was yet a child, and wholly unacquainted with the manners of the world; yet, young as I was, I became the traveller of its mazy and perilous paths. At an age when girls are generally at school, or indeed scarcely emancipated from the nursery, I was presented in society as a wife–and very nearly as a mother.

Lord Lyttelton, who was perhaps the most accomplished libertine that any age or country has produced, with considerable artifice inquired after Mr. Robinson, professed his earnest desire to cultivate his acquaintance, and, on the following day, sent him a card of invitation. Lyttelton was an adept in the artifices of fashionable intrigue. He plainly perceived that both Mr. Robinson and myself were uninitiated in its mysteries; he knew that to undermine a wife's honour he must become master of the husband's confidence, and Mr. Robinson was too much pleased with the society of a man whose wit was only equalled by his profligacy, to shrink from such an association.

Fortunately for me, Lord Lyttelton was uniformly my aversion. His manners were overbearingly insolent, his language licentious, and his person slovenly even to a degree that was disgusting. Mr. Robinson was in every respect the very reverse of his companion: he was unassuming, neat, and delicate in his conversation. I had not a wish to descend from the propriety of wedded life, and I abhorred, decidedly abhorred, the acquaintance with Lord Lyttelton.

In the course of a few days his lordship presented me the works of Miss Aitken [1] (now Mrs. Barbauld). I read them with rapture. I thought them the most beautiful poems I had ever seen, and considered the woman who could invent such poetry as the most to be envied of human creatures. Lord Lyttelton had some taste for poetical compositions, and wrote verses with considerable facility.

On the following Monday I again visited the Pantheon. My dress was then white and silver. Again I was followed with attention. Lord Lyttelton was my *cavaliere servente* that evening, though, as usual, his chief attention was paid to Mr. Robinson. During the concert he presented the Count de Belgeioso, the Imperial Ambassador, one of the most accomplished foreigners I ever remember having met with. Lord Valentia was also introduced, but as his lordship had recently made some *èclat* by his attentions to the celebrated Mrs. Elliot, I rather avoided than wished to cultivate his acquaintance.

Mr. Robinson's intercourse with the world was now rapidly augmenting. Every day was productive of some new association. Lord Lyttelton presented many of his friends; among others, Captain O'Byrne, and Mr. William Brereton, of Drury Lane Theatre. In the course of a short time we also became acquainted with Sir Francis Molyneux, Mr. Alderman Sayer, and the late unfortunate George Robert Fitzgerald. [1] Lord Northington was also a constant visitor, and frequently rallied me on what he thought my striking likeness to his family.

Among my female friends, those for whom I entertained the strongest esteem were Lady Yea, the wife of Sir William Yea, and the sister of Sir John Trevellyan. She was a lovely and accomplished woman. Mrs. Parry, the wife of the Rev. Dr. Parry, and the author of "Eden Vale," a novel, was also one of my most favourite acquaintances. Mrs. Parry was a woman of considerable talents, a wit, and of remarkably pleasing manners.

Of those who frequented our house Lord Lyttelton was most decidedly my abhorrence; I knew that he frequently led my husband from the paths of domestic confidence to the haunts of profligate debasement. Towards me his lordship affected great indifference. He has even in my presence declared that no woman under thirty years of age was worth admiring; that even the antiquity of forty was far preferable to the insipidity of sixteen; and he generally concluded his observations by hoping he had not made *"The pretty child angry."*

I soon discovered that his intercourse with Lord Lyttelton produced a very considerable change in Mr. Robinson's domestic deportment. They were constantly together, and the neglect which I experienced began to alarm me. I dedicated all my leisure hours to poetry; I wrote verses of all sorts; and Mr. Robinson having mentioned that I had proposed appearing on the stage previous to my marriage in the character of Cordelia, Lord Lyttelton facetiously christened me the Poetess Corry.

It was with extreme regret, and frequently with uncontrollable indignation, that I endured the neglect of my husband and the tauntings of the profligate Lyttelton. "The child"–for so he generally called me–was deserted for the society of the most libertine men and the most abandoned women. Mr. Robinson became not only careless of his wife, but of his pecuniary finances, while I was kept in total ignorance as to the resources which supported his increasing expenses.

Among my other friends, Lady Yea frequently inquired by what means my husband supported his household disbursements. Our table was elegantly, though not profusely, served. Mr. Robinson seldom attended to his profession, and I was too young, as well as too inexperienced, to look after family affairs. My younger brother George, whom upon my marriage Mr. Robinson and myself adopted as our own, now finding his health impaired, my mother attended him at Bristol, so that I had no friend to advise me who felt any real interest in my welfare. Dress, parties, adulation, occupied all my hours. Mr. Robinson's easy temper was influenced by the counsel of his friend Lyttelton, and he every hour sunk more deeply in the gulf of dissipation.

Among the most dangerous of my husband's associates was George Robert Fitzgerald. His manners towards women were interesting and attentive. He perceived the neglect with which I was treated by Mr. Robinson, and the pernicious influence which Lord Lyttelton had acquired over his mind; he professed to feel the warmest interest in my welfare, lamented the destiny which had befallen me in being wedded to a man incapable of estimating my value, and at last confessed *himself* my most ardent and devoted admirer. I shuddered at the declaration, for, amidst all the allurements of splendid folly, my mind, the purity of my virtue, was still uncontaminated.

I repulsed the dangerous advances of this accomplished person, but I did not the less feel the humiliation to which a husband's indifference had exposed me. God can bear witness to the purity of my soul, even surrounded by temptations and mortified by neglect. Whenever I ventured to inquire into pecuniary resources, Mr. Robinson silenced me by saying that he was independent; added to this assurance, Lord Lyttelton repeatedly promised that, through his courtly interest, he would very shortly obtain for my husband some honourable and lucrative situation.

I confess that I reposed but little confidence in the promises of such a man, though my husband believed them inviolable. Frequent parties were made at his lordship's house in Hill Street, and many invitations pressed for a visit to his seat at Hagley. These I peremptorily refused, till the noble hypocrite became convinced of my aversion, and adopted a new mode of pursuing his machinations.

One forenoon Lord Lyttelton called in Hatton Garden, as was almost his daily custom, and, on finding that Mr. Robinson was not at home, requested to speak with me on business of importance. I found him seemingly much distressed. He informed me that he had a secret to communicate of considerable moment both to my interest and happiness. I started.

"Nothing, I trust in heaven, has befallen my husband!" said I, with a voice scarcely articulate.

Lord Lyttelton hesitated.

"How little does that husband deserve the solicitude of such a wife!" said he; "but," continued his lordship, "I fear that I have in some degree aided in alienating his conjugal affections. I could not bear to see such youth, such merit, so sacrificed—"

"Speak briefly, my lord," said I.

"Then," replied Lord Lyttelton, "I must inform you that your husband is the most false and undeserving of that name! He has formed a connection with a woman of abandoned character; he lavishes on her those means of subsistence which you will shortly stand in need of."

"I do not believe it," said I, indignantly.

"Then you shall be convinced," answered his lordship; "but remember, if you betray me, your true and zealous friend, I must fight your husband; for he never will forgive my having discovered his infidelity."

"It cannot be true," said I. "You have been misinformed."

"Then it has been by the woman who usurps your place in the affections of your husband," replied Lord Lyttelton. "From her I received the information. Her name is Harriet Wilmot; she resides in Soho. Your husband daily visits her."

I thought I should have fainted; but a torrent of tears recalled the ebbing current of my heart, and I grew proud in fortitude, though humbled in self-love.

"Now," said Lord Lyttelton, "if you are a woman of spirit, you will be *revenged!* " I shrunk with horror, and would have quitted the room. "Hear me," said he. "You cannot be a stranger to my motives for thus cultivating the friendship of your husband. My fortune is at your disposal. Robinson is a ruined man; his debts are considerable, and nothing but destruction can await you. Leave him! Command my powers to serve you."

I would hear no more–broke from him, and rushed out of the apartments. My sensations, my sufferings were indescribable.

I immediately took a hackney coach, and proceeded to Prince's Street, Soho –Lord Lyttelton having given me the address of my rival. Language cannot describe what I suffered till I arrived at the lodgings of Miss Wilmot. The coachman knocked, a dirty servant girl opened the door. Her mistress was not at home. I quitted the coach and ascended to the drawing-room, where the servant left me, after informing me that Miss W. would return in a very short time. I was now left alone.

I opened the chamber-door which led from the drawing-room; a new white lustring sacque and petticoat lay on the bed. While I was examining the room, a loud knocking at the street door alarmed me. I re-entered the front apartment, and waited with a palpitating bosom till the being whose triumph had awakened both my pride and my resentment appeared before me.

She was a handsome woman, though evidently some years older than myself. She wore a dress of printed Irish muslin, with a black gauze cloak and a chip hat, trimmed with pale lilac ribbons; she was tall, and had a very pleasing countenance. Her manner was timid and confused; her lips as pale as ashes. I commiserated her distress, desired her not to be alarmed, and we took our seats, with increased composure.

"I came to inquire whether or not you are acquainted with a Mr. Robinson," said I.

"I am," replied Miss Wilmot. "He visits me frequently." She drew off her glove as she spoke, and passing her hand over her eyes, I observed on her finger a ring, which I knew to have been my husband's.

"I have nothing more to say," added I, "but to request that you will favour me with Mr. Robinson's address; I have something which I wish to convey to him."

She smiled, and cast her eyes over my figure. My dress was a morning *dèshabill* of India muslin, with a bonnet of straw, and a white lawn cloak bordered with lace.

"You are Mr. Robinson's wife," said she, with a trembling voice. "I am sure you are; and probably this ring was yours; pray receive it–"

I declined taking the ring. She continued, "Had I known that Mr. Robinson was the husband of such a woman–"

I rose to leave her. She added, "I never will see him more–unworthy man–I never will again receive him."

I could make no reply, but rose and departed.

On my return to Hatton Garden I found my husband waiting dinner. I concealed my chagrin. We had made a party that evening to Drury Lane Theatre, and from thence to a select concert at the Count de Belgeioso's, in Portman Square. Lord Lyttelton was to join us at both places. We went to the play; but my agitation had produced such a violent headache that I was obliged to send an apology for not keeping our engagement at the Imperial Ambassador's.

On the following morning I spoke to Mr. Robinson respecting Miss Wilmot. He did not deny that he knew such a person; that he had visited her; but he threw all the blame of his indiscretion on Lord

Lyttelton. He requested to know who had informed me of his conduct. I refused to tell; and he had too high an opinion of his false associate to suspect him of such treachery.

At one of Mrs. Parry's card parties I met Mrs. Abington. [1] I thought her the most lively and bewitching woman I had ever seen; her manners were fascinating, and the peculiar tastefulness of her dress excited universal admiration. My imagination again wandered to the stage, and I thought the heroine of the scenic art was of all human creatures the most to be envied.

About this period I observed that Mr. Robinson had frequent visitors of the Jewish tribe; that he was often closeted with them, and that some secret negotiation was going forward to which I was a total stranger. Among others, Mr. King was a constant visitor; indeed he had often been with my husband on private business ever since the period of our marriage. I questioned Mr. Robinson upon the subject of these strange and repeated interviews. He assured me that the persons I had seen came merely upon law business, and that in his profession it was necessary to be civil to all ranks of people. Whenever I urged a farther explanation he assumed a tone of displeasure, and requested me not to meddle with his professional occupations. I desisted; and the parlour of our house was almost as much frequented by Jews as though it had been their synagogue.

Mr. Robinson's mornings were devoted to his bearded friends, his evenings to his fashionable associates; but my hours were all dedicated to sorrow, for I now heard that my husband, even at the period of his marriage, had an attachment which he had not broken, and that his infidelities were as public as the ruin of his finances was inevitable. I remonstrated–I was almost frantic. My distress was useless, my wishes to retrench our expenses ineffectual. Mr. Robinson had, *Previous to our union* deeply involved himself in a bond debt of considerable magnitude, and he had from time to time borrowed money on annuity–one sum to discharge the other–till every plan of liquidation appeared impracticable. During all this time my mother was at Bristol.

Lord Lyttelton, finding every plan of seduction fail, now rested his only hope of subduing my honour in the certainty of my husband's ruin. He therefore took every step embraced every opportunity of involving him more deeply in calamity. Parties were made to Richmond and Salt Hill, to Ascot Heath and Epsom races, in all of which Mr. Robinson bore his share of expense, with the addition of post-horses. Whenever he seemed to shrink from his augmenting indiscretion, Lord Lyttelton assured him that, through his interest, an appointment of honourable and pecuniary importance should be obtained, though I embraced every opportunity to assure his lordship that no consideration upon earth should ever make me the victim of his artifice.

Mr. Fitzgerald still paid me unremitting attention. His manners *towards women* were beautifully interesting. He frequently cautioned me against the libertine Lyttelton, and as frequently lamented the misguided confidence which Mr. Robinson reposed in him. Lord Lyttelton's shameless conduct towards an amiable wife, from whom he was separated, and his cruel neglect of a lady of the name of Dawson, who had long been attached to him, marked the unworthiness of his character. He was the very last man in the world for whom I ever could have entertained the smallest partiality; he was to me the most hateful of existing beings. Probably these pages will be read when the hand that writes them moulders in the grave, when that God who judges all hearts will know how innocent I was of the smallest conjugal infidelity. I make this solemn asseveration because there have been malevolent spirits who, in the plenitude of their calumny, have slandered me by suspecting my fidelity even at this early period of my existence. These pages are the pages of truth, unadorned by romance and unembellished by the graces of phraseology, and I know that I have been sufficiently the victim of events too well to become the tacit acquiescer where I have been grossly misrepresented. Alas! Of all created beings I have been the most severely subjugated by circumstances more than by inclination.

About this time a party was one evening made to Vauxhall. Mr. Fitzgerald was the person who proposed it, and it consisted of six or eight persons. The night was warm and the gardens crowded. We supped in the circle which has the statue of Handel in its centre. The hour growing, late–or rather early in the morning–our company dispersed, and no one remained excepting Mr. Robinson, Mr. Fitzgerald, and myself. Suddenly a noise was heard near the orchestra. A crowd had assembled, and two gentlemen were quarrelling furiously. Mr. R. and Fitzgerald ran out of the box. I rose to follow them, but they were lost in the throng, and I thought it most prudent to resume my place, which I had just quitted, as the only certain way of their finding me in safety. In a moment Fitzgerald returned. "Robinson," said he, "is gone to seek you at the entrance-door. He thought you had quitted the box."

Mrs Robinson
from an Engraving by Dickinson after Reynolds.

"I did for a moment," said I, "but I was fearful of losing him in the crowd, and therefore returned."

"Let me conduct you to the door; we shall certainly find him there," replied Mr. Fitzgerald. "I know that he will be uneasy. "

I took his arm, and we ran hastily towards the entrance-door on the Vauxhall Road.

Mr. Robinson was not there. We proceeded to look for our carriage. It stood at some distance. I was alarmed and bewildered. Mr. Fitzgerald hurried me along. "Don't be uneasy; we shall certainly find him," said he "for I left him here not five minutes ago." As he spoke he stopped abruptly. A servant opened a chaise door. There were four horses harnessed to it; and by the light of the lamps on the side of the footpath I plainly perceived a pistol in the pocket of the door which was open. I drew back. Mr. Fitzgerald placed his arm round my waist, and endeavoured to lift me up the step of the chaise, the servant watching at a little distance. I resisted, and inquired what he meant by such conduct. His hand trembled excessively, while he said in a low voice, "Robinson can but fight me." I was terrified beyond all description. I made him loose his hold, and ran towards the entrance-door. Mr. Fitzgerald now perceived Mr. Robinson. "Here he comes!" exclaimed he, with easy *nonchalance* "We had found the wrong carriage, Mr. Robinson. We have been looking after you, and Mrs. Robinson is alarmed beyond expression."

"I am indeed!" said I. Mr. Robinson now took my hand. We stepped into the coach, and Mr. Fitzgerald followed. As we proceeded towards Hatton Garden the sky incessantly flashed lightning. I was terrified by the combination of events, and I was in a situation which rendered any alarm peculiarly dangerous, for I was several months advanced in that state which afterwards terminated by presenting to me my only child, my *darling* Maria. [1]

I had often heard of Mr. Fitzgerald's propensity to duelling. I recollected my own delicate situation; I valued my husband's safety. I therefore did not mention the adventure of the evening, particularly as Mr. Fitzgerald observed, on our way to Hatton Garden, that he had "nearly made a strange mistake, and taken possession of another person's carriage." This remark appeared so plausible that nothing farther was said upon the subject.

From that evening I was particularly cautious in avoiding Fitzgerald. He was too daring and too fascinating a being to be allowed the smallest marks of confidence. Whenever he called I was denied to him, and at length, perceiving the impracticability of his plan, he desisted, and seldom called, excepting to leave his name as a visitor of ceremony.

I do not recount these events, these plans for my enthralment, with a view to convey anything like personal vanity, for I can with truth affirm that I never thought myself entitled to admiration that could endanger my security or tempt the libertine to undermine my husband's honour. But I attribute the snares that were laid for me to three causes: the first, my youth and inexperience, my girlish appearance and simplicity of manners; secondly, the expensive style in which Mr. Robinson lived, though he was not known as a man of independent fortune; and thirdly, the evident neglect which I experienced from my husband, whom Lord Lyttelton's society had marked as a man of universal gallantry.

I was now known by name at every public place in and near the metropolis. Our circle of acquaintances enlarged daily. My friend Lady Yea was my constant companion. Mr. Robinson became desperate, from a thorough conviction that no effort of economy or professional labour could arrange his shattered finances, the large debt which he owed *previous to his marriage to* me having laid the foundation of every succeeding embarrassment.

The moment now approached when the arcanum was to be developed, and an execution on Mr. Robinson's effects, at the suit of an annuitant, decided the doubts and fears which had long afflicted me. I was in a great degree prepared for this event by the evident inquietude of my husband's mind and his frequent interviews with persons of a mysterious description. Indeed this crisis seemed rather consolatory than appalling, for I hoped and trusted that the time was now arrived when reason would take place of folly, and experience point out those thorns which strew the pleasurable paths of dissipation.

At this period, had Mr. Harris generously assisted *his son I am fully and confidently persuaded that he would have pursued a discreet and regular line of conduct.* His *first* involvement was the basis of all his misfortunes. The impossibility of liquidating that debt (the motive for which it was contracted is to this hour unknown to me) rendered him desperate. Indeed, how could a young man, well educated, [1] subsist in such a metropolis without some provision? Mr. Harris was a man of fortune, and he ought to have known that necessity is the most dangerous associate of youth; that folly may be reclaimed by kindness, but seldom fails to be darkened into vice by the severity of unpitying natures.

From Hatton Garden we removed to a house which was lent to us by a friend at Finchley. Here I hoped at least to remain tranquil till the perilous moment was passed which was to render me a mother. I here devoted my time to making my infant's little wardrobe; my finest muslin dresses I converted into frocks and robes, with my lace I fondly trimmed them. It was a sweetly pleasing task, and I often smiled when I reflected that only three years before this period I had dressed a waxen doll nearly as large as a newborn infant.

Mr. Robinson had much business to transact in London, and I was almost perpetually alone at Finchley. Of our domestic establishment there was only one who did not desert us, and he was a negro!–one of that despised, degraded race, who wear the colour on their features which too often characterises the hearts of their fair and unfeeling oppressors. I have found, during my journey through life, that the two male domestics who were most attached to my interest and most faithful to my fortunes were both *negroes!*

My mother now returned from Bristol, and I had the consolation of her society. I divided my time betwixt reading, writing, and making a little wardrobe for my expected darling. I little regretted the busy scenes of life; I sighed not for public attention. I felt by this change of situation as though a weighty load were taken from my heart, and solaced my mind in the idea that the worst had happened which could befall us. Gracious Heaven! How should I have shuddered, had I then contemplated the dark perspective of my destiny!

Mr. Robinson went almost daily to London, and sometimes my brother George, who was still a boy, accompanied him upon a little pony. One day, after returning from one of their rides, my brother informed me that he had been with Mr. Robinson to Marylebone, and that he had waited and held Mr. Robinson's horse, while he made a morning visit. I had then no acquaintance that resided at Marylebone. I questioned my brother as to the place, and he persisted in his original story. "But," added he, "if you say anything about it to Mr. Robinson, I never will tell you where we go in future." I promised not to mention what he had said, and my mind was deeply engaged in a variety of conjectures.

A few days after Mr. Robinson made another visit, and my brother was introduced to the lady. From the manner and conversation of both parties, even a youth scarcely in his teens could draw conclusions of no favourable nature. By the side of the chimney hung my watch, which I had supposed lost in the general wreck of our property. It was enamelled with musical trophies, and very remarkable for a steel chain of singular beauty. The moment my brother described it my suspicions were confirmed; and Mr. Robinson did not even attempt to deny his infidelity.

Mr. Robinson, finding his creditors inexorable, and fearing that he might endanger his personal liberty by remaining near London, informed me that I must, in a few days, accompany him to Tregunter. I felt a severe pang in the idea of quitting my adored mother at a moment when I should stand so much in need of a parent's attentions. My agony was extreme. I fancied that I never should behold her more; that the harshness and humiliating taunts of my husband's kindred would send me prematurely to the grave; that my infant would be left among strangers, and that my mother would scarcely have fortitude sufficient to survive me. Then I anticipated the inconvenience of so long a journey, for Tregunter House was within a few miles of Brecon. I dreaded to encounter the scornful vulgarity and the keen glances of Miss Betsy and Mrs. Molly. I considered all these things with horror; but the propriety of wedded life commanded the sacrifice, and I readily consented to make it.

49

With tender regret, with agonising presentiments, I took leave of my mother and my brother. Such a parting would but mock the powers of language! My delicate situation, my youth, my affection for my best of mothers, all conspired to augment my sorrow–but a husband's repose, a husband's *liberty* were at stake, and my Creator can bear witness that, had I been blessed with that fidelity and affection which I deserved, my heart was disposed to the observance of every duty, every claim which would have embellished domestic propriety.

We set out for Tregunter. On our arrival there, I instantly perceived that our misfortunes had outstripped our speed. Miss Robinson scarcely bade us welcome, and Molly was peevish, even to insulting displeasure.

Mr. Harris was from home when we arrived. But he returned shortly after. His greeting was harsh and unfeeling. "Well! so you have escaped from a prison, and now you are come here to do penance for your follies? Well! and what do you want?" I could not reply. I entered the house, and instantly hastened to my old chamber, where my tears gave relief to that heart which was almost bursting with agony.

Still Mr. Robinson conjured me to bear his *uncles* wayward temper patiently. I did, though every day I was taunted with idle and inhuman questions, such as, "How long do you think that I will support you? What is to become of you in a prison? What business have beggars to marry?" With many others, equally feeling and high-minded!

The mansion of Tregunter presented but few sources of amusement for the female mind. Mr. Harris had acquired a considerable fortune in trade, and, however the art of accumulating wealth had been successfully practised, the finer pursuits of mental powers had been totally neglected. Books were unknown at Tregunter, excepting a few magazines or periodical publications, which at different periods Miss Robinson borrowed from her juvenile neighbours. There was, however, an old spinnet in one of the parlours. Music had been one of my early delights, and I sometimes vainly endeavoured to draw a kind of jingling harmony from this time-shaken and neglected instrument. These attempts, however, frequently subjected me to insult. "I had better think of getting my bread; women of no fortune had no right to follow the pursuits of fine ladies. Tom had better married a good tradesman's daughter than the child of a ruined merchant who was not capable of earning a living." Such were the remarks of my amiable and enlightened father-in-law!

One day, I particularly remember, Mr. Harris had invited a large party to dinner. John and Charles Morgan, Esqrs., members of Parliament, with an old clergyman of the name of Jones, and several others were present. I was then within a fortnight of my perilous moment. One of the company expressed his satisfaction that I was come to give Tregunter a little stranger; and turning to Mr. Harris, added–

"You have just finished your house in time for a nursery."

"No, no," replied Mr. Harris, laughing, "they came here because *prison doors* were open to receive them."

I felt my face redden to scarlet; every person present seemed to sympathise in my chagrin, and I was near sinking under the table with confusion. Mr. Robinson's indignation was evident; but it was restrained by duty as well as by necessity.

The manor-house was not yet finished; and a few days after our arrival Mr. Harris informed me that he had no accommodation for my approaching confinement. Where was I to go? was the next question. After many family consultations, it was decided that I should remove to Trevecca House, about a mile and a half distant, and there give to this miserable world my first-born darling.

I removed to Trevecca; it was a spacious mansion at the foot of a stupendous mountain, which, from its form, was called the Sugar-loaf. A part of the building was converted into a flannel manufactory, and the inhabitants were of the Huntingdonian school.

Here I enjoyed the sweet repose of solitude; here I wandered about woods entangled by the wild luxuriance of nature, or roved upon the mountain's side, while the blue vapours floated round its summit. Oh, God of Nature! Sovereign of the universe of wonders! in those interesting moments how fervently did I adore thee! '

How often have I sat at my little parlour window and watched the pale moonbeams darting amidst the sombre and venerable yew-trees that shed their solemn shade over the little garden! How often have I strolled down the woody paths, spangled with the dew of morning, and shaken off the briery branches that hung about me! How tranquil did I feel escaped from kindred tyranny, and how little did I regret the busy scenes of fashionable folly! Unquestionably the Creator formed me with a strong propensity to adore the sublime and beautiful of His works! But it has never been my lot to meet with an associating mind, a congenial spirit, who could (as it were abstracted from the world), find an universe in the sacred intercourse of soul, the sublime union of sensibility.

At Trevecca House I was tranquil, if not perfectly happy. I there avoided the low taunts of uncultivated natures, the insolent vulgarity of pride, and the overbearing triumphs of a family, *whose lofliest branch* was as inferior to *my stock* as the *small weeds* is beneath the *tallest tree* that overshades it. I had formed a union with a family who had neither sentiment nor sensibility; I was doomed to bear the society of ignorance and pride; I was treated as though I had been the most abject of beings, even at a time when my conscious spirit soared as far above their powers to wound it as the mountain towered over the white battlements of my then solitary habitation.

After my removal to Trevecca, I seldom saw Miss Robinson or Mrs. Molly; Mr. Harris never called on me, though I was not more than a mile and a half from Tregunter. At length the expected, though to me most perilous, moment arrived, which awoke a new and tender interest in my bosom, which presented to my fondly beating heart my child—my Maria. I cannot describe the sensations of my soul at the moment when I pressed the little darling to my bosom, my maternal bosom; when I kissed its hands, its cheeks, its forehead, as it nestled closely to my heart, and seemed to claim that affection which has never failed to warm it. She was the most beautiful of infants! I thought myself the happiest of mothers; her first smile appeared like something celestial–something ordained to irradiate my dark and dreary prospect of existence.

Two days after my child was presented to this world of sorrow, my nurse, Mrs. Jones, a most excellent woman, was earnestly desired by the people of the manufactory to bring the infant among them; they wished to see the "young squire's baby, the little *hieress* to Tregunter." It was in vain that I dreaded the consequences of the visit, for it was in the month of October; but Mrs. Jones assured me that infants in that part of the world were very frequently carried into the open air on the day of their birth: she also hinted that my refusal would hurt the feelings of the honest people, and wear the semblance of pride more than of maternal tenderness. This idea decided my acquiescence; and my little darling, enveloped in the manufacture of her own romantic birthplace, made her first visit to her kind but unsophisticated countrywomen.

No sooner did Mrs. Jones enter the circle than she was surrounded by the gazing throng. The infant was dressed with peculiar neatness, and nothing mortal could appear more lovely. A thousand and a thousand blessings were heaped upon the "of Tregunter," for so they *fancifully* called her; a thousand times did they declare that the baby was the very image of her father. Mrs. Jones returned to me; every word she uttered soothed my heart; a sweet and grateful glow, for the first time, bespoke the indescribable gratification which a fond parent feels in hearing the praises of a beloved offspring. Yet this little absence appeared an age; a variety of fears presented dangers in a variety of shapes, and the object of all my care, of all my affection, was now pressed closer to my heart than ever.

Amidst these sweet and never-to-be-forgotten sensations, Mr. Harris entered my chamber. He abruptly inquired how I found myself, and, seating himself by the side of my bed, began to converse on family affairs. I was too feeble to say much; and he had not the delicacy to consider that Mrs. Jones, my nurse, and almost a stranger to me, was a witness to our conversation.

"Well!" said Mr. Harris, "and what do you mean to do with your child?"

I made no answer.

"I will tell you," added he. "Tie it to your back and work for it."

I shivered with horror.

"Prison doors are open," continued Mr. Harris. "Tom will die in a gaol; and what is to become of you?"

I remained silent.

Miss Robinson now made her visit. She looked at me without uttering a syllable; but while she contemplated my infant's features, her innocent sleeping face, her little dimpled hands folded on her breast, she murmured, " Poor little wretch! Poor thing! It would be a mercy if it pleased God to take it!" My agony of mind was scarcely supportable.

About three weeks after this period letters arrived, informing Mr. Robinson that his creditors were still inexorable, and that the place of his concealment was known. He was cautioned not to run the hazard of an arrest; indeed he knew that such an event would complete his ruin with Mr. Harris, from whom he should not receive any assistance. He communicated this intelligence to me, and at the same time informed me that he must absolutely depart from Trevecca immediately. I was still extremely feeble, for my mental sufferings had impaired my corporeal strength almost as much as the perils I had recently encountered. But the idea of remaining at Trevecca without my husband was more terrible than the prospect of annihilation, and I replied without a hesitating thought, "I am ready to go with you."

My good nurse, who was a very amiable woman, and under forty years of age, conjured me to delay my journey. She informed me that it would be dangerous to undertake it in my then weak state. My husband's liberty was in danger, and my life appeared of little importance; for even at that early period of my days I was already weary of existence.

On the succeeding morning we departed. Mrs. Jones insisted on accompanying me on the first day's journey. Mr. Robinson, my nurse, and myself occupied a post-chaise; my Maria was placed on a pillow on Mrs. Jones's lap. The paleness of death overspread my countenance, and the poor honest people of the mountains and the villages saw us depart with sorrow, though not without their blessings. Neither Mr. Harris nor the *enlightened females* of Tregunter expressed the smallest regret or solicitude on the occasion. We reached Abergavenny that evening. My little remaining strength was exhausted, and I could proceed no further. However singular these persecutions may appear, Mr. Robinson knows that they are not in the smallest degree exaggerated.

At Abergavenny I parted from Mrs. Jones, and, having no domestic with me, was left to take the entire charge of Maria. Reared in the tender lap of affluence, I had learnt but little of domestic occupations; the adorning part of education had been lavished, but the useful had never been bestowed upon a girl who was considered as born to independence. With these disadvantages I felt very awkwardly situated, under the arduous task I had to perform; but necessity soon prevailed with the soft voice of maternal affection, and I obeyed her dictates as the dictates of nature.

Mrs. Jones, whose excellent heart sympathised in all I suffered, would not have parted from me in so delicate a moment, but she was the widow of a tradesman at Brecon, and having quitted her home, where she had left two daughters–very pretty young women–to attend me, she was under the necessity of returning to them. With repeated good wishes, and some tears of regret flowing from her feeling and gentle heart, we parted.

On the following day we proceeded to Monmouth. Some relations of my mother residing there, particularly my grandmother, I wished to remain there till my strength was somewhat restored. We were received with genuine affection; we were caressed with unfeigned hospitality. The good and venerable object of my visit was delighted to embrace her *great-grandchild* and the family fireside was frequently a scene of calm and pleasing conversation. How different were these moments from those which I had passed with the low-minded inhabitants of Tregunter!

My grandmother, though then near seventy years of age, was still a pleasing woman; she had in her youth been delicately beautiful: and the neat simplicity of her dress, which was always either brown or black silk, the piety of her mind, and the mildness of her nature, combined to render her a most endearing object.

As soon as my strength recovered I was invited to partake of many pleasant entertainments. But the most favourite amusement I selected was that of wandering by the river Wye, or of exploring the antique remains of Monmouth Castle, a part of which reached the garden of my grandmother's habitation. I also constantly accompanied my amiable and venerable relative to church; and I have often observed, with a mixture of delight, and *almost* of envy, the tranquil resignation which religion diffused over her mind, even at the very close of human existence. This excellent woman expired of a gradual decay in the year 1780.

We had resided at Monmouth about a month, when I was invited to a ball. My spirits and strength had been renovated by the change of scenery, and I was persuaded to dance. I was at that time particularly fond of the amusement, and my partial friends flattered me by saying that I measured the mazy figure like a sylph. I was at that period a nurse; and, during the evening, Maria was brought to an antechamber to receive the only support she had ever yet taken. Unconscious of the danger attendant on such an event, I gave her her accustomed nourishment immediately after dancing. It was agitated by the violence of exercise and the heat of the ball-room, and, on my return home, I found my infant in strong convulsions.

My distraction, my despair, was terrible; my state of mind rendered it impossible for me to afford any internal nourishment to the child, even when her little mouth was parched, or the fit in the smallest degree abated. I was little less than frantic; all the night I sat with her on my arms; an eminent medical man attended. The convulsions continued, and my situation was terrible; those who witnessed it cautiously avoided informing me that the peril of my infant proceeded from my dancing; had I known it at that period I really believe I should have lost my senses.

In this desperate state, with only short intervals of rest, my darling continued till the morning. All my friends came to make inquiries, and, among others, a clergyman who visited at my grandmother's. He saw the child, as it was thought, expiring; he saw me still sitting where I had taken my place of despair on the preceding night, fixed in the stupor of unutterable affliction. He conjured me to let the child be removed. I was in a raging fever; the effects of not having nourished my child during twelve hours began to endanger my own existence, and I looked forward to my dissolution as the happiest event that could befall me.

Still Maria lay upon my lap, and still I resisted every attempt that was made to remove her. Just at this period the clergyman recollected that he had seen one of his children relieved from convulsions by a simple experiment, and he requested my permission to try its effects. The child was given over by my medical attendant, and I replied, "However desperate the remedy, I conjure you to administer it."

He now mixed a tablespoonful of spirit of aniseed with a small quantity of spermacetti, and gave it to my infant. In a few minutes the convulsive spasms abated, and in less than an hour she sunk into a sweet and tranquil slumber. What I felt may be pictured to a fond *mother's* fancy, but my pen would fail in attempting to describe it.

Some circumstances now occurred which gave Mr. Robinson reason to believe that he was not safe at Monmouth, and we prepared for a removal to some other quarter. The day was fixed for commencing our journey, when an execution arrived for a considerable sum, and Mr. Robinson was no longer at liberty to travel. My alarm was infinite; the sum was too large for the possibility of liquidation, and, knowing Mr. Robinson's desperate fortune, I thought it unjust as well as ungenerous to attempt the borrowing of it. Fortunately the sheriff for the county was a friend of the family. He was a gentlemanly and amiable man, and offered–to avoid any unpleasant dilemma–to accompany us to London. We set out the same evening, and never slept till we arrived in the metropolis.

I immediately hastened to my mother, who resided in Buckingham Street, York Buildings, now the Adelphi. Her joy was boundless. She kissed me a thousand times, she kissed my beautiful infant; while Mr. Robinson employed the day in accommodating the business which had brought him to London. He had been arrested by a friend, with a hope that, so near a father's habitation, such a sum would have been paid–at least such is the reason assigned for such unfriendly conduct! [1]

The matter was, however, arranged on an explanation taking place, and Mr. Robinson engaged lodging near Berners Street, whither we repaired on the same evening. My little collection of poems, which I had arranged for publication, and which had been ready ever since my marriage, I now determined to print immediately. They were indeed trifles, very trifles; I have since perused them with a blush of self-reproof, and wondered how I could venture on presenting them to the public. I trust that there is not a copy remaining, excepting that which my dear partial mother fondly preserved, and which is now in my possession.

I had been in town a few days, when some female friends persuaded me to accompany a party which they had formed to Ranelagh. Mr. Robinson declined going, but after much entreaty I consented. I had now been married near two years; my person was considerably improved; I was grown taller than when I became Mr. Robinson's wife, and I had now more the manners of a woman of the world than those of girlish simplicity, which had hitherto characterised me, though I had been some months absent from London, and a part of them rusticated among mountains. The dress which I wore was plain and simple: it was composed of pale lilac lustring. My head had a wreath of white flowers; I was complimented on my looks by the whole party, and with little relish for public amusements, and a heart throbbing with domestic solicitude, I accompanied the party to Ranelagh.

The first person I saw on entering the rotunda was George Robert Fitzgerald. He started as if he had received a shock of electricity. I turned my head away, and would have avoided him; but he instantly quitted two friends with whom he was walking, and presented himself to me. He expressed great pleasure at seeing me once more in "the world "; was surprised at finding me for the *first time* in public without my husband, and requested permission to pay his respects to me at my house. I replied that I was "on a visit to some friends." He bowed, and rejoined his companions.

During the evening, however, he never ceased to follow me. We quitted the rotunda early; and, as we were waiting for the carriage, I again observed Fitzgerald in the antechamber. We passed the vestibule, and at the door his own carriage was waiting.

On the following noon I was correcting a proof-sheet of my volume, when the servant abruptly announced Mr. Fitzgerald!

I was somewhat disconcerted by this unexpected visit, and received Mr. Fitzgerald with a cold and embarrassed mien, which evidently mortified him; I also felt a little worldly vanity in the moment of surprise, for my morning dress was more calculated to display maternal assiduity than elegant and tasteful *dèshabille* In a small basket near my chair slept my little Maria; my table was spread with papers, and everything around me presented the mixed confusion of a study and a nursery.

From the period of Mrs. Jones's quitting me at Abergavenny, I had made it an invariable rule always to dress and undress my infant. I never suffered it to be placed in a cradle, or to be fed out of my presence. A basket of an oblong shape with four handles (with a pillow and a small bolster) was her bed by day; at night she slept with me. I had too often heard of the neglect which servants show to young children, and I resolved never to expose an infant of mine either to their ignorance or inattention. It was amidst the duties of a parent, that the gay, the high-fashioned Fitzgerald now found me; and whenever either business or, very rarely, public amusements drew me from the occupation, my mother never failed to be my substitute.

Mr. Fitzgerald said a thousand civil things; but that which charmed me, was the admiration of my child. He declared that he had never seen so young a mother, or so beautiful an infant. For the first remark I sighed, but the last delighted my bosom; she indeed was one of the prettiest little mortals that ever the sun shone upon.

The next subject of praise was my poetry. I smile while I recollect how far the effrontery of flattery has power to belie the judgment. Mr. Fitzgerald took up the proof-sheet and read one of the pastorals. I inquired by what means he had discovered my place of residence; he informed me that his carriage had followed me home on the preceding night. He now took his leave.

On the following evening he made us another visit; I say us, because Mr. Robinson was at home. Mr. Fitzgerald drank tea with us, and proposed making a party on the next day to dine at Richmond. To this I gave a decided negative; alleging that my duty towards my child prevented the possibility of passing a day absent from her.

On the Wednesday following Mr. Robinson accompanied me again to Ranelagh. There we met Lord Northington, Lord Lyttelton, Captain O'Bryan, Captain Ayscough, Mr. Andrews, and several others, who all, in the course of the evening, evinced their attentions. But as Mr. Robinson's deranged state of affairs did not admit of our receiving parties at home, I made my excuses by saying that we were at a friend's house and not yet established in a town resi- dence. Lord Lyttelton was particularly importunate; but he received the same answer which I had given to every other inquirer.

A short time after Mr. Robinson was arrested. Now came my hour of trial. He was conveyed to the house of a sheriff's officer, and in a few days detainers were lodged against him to the amount of twelve hundred pounds, chiefly the arrears of annuities and other demands from Jew creditors; for I can proudly and with truth declare that he did not at that time, or at any period since, owe fifty pounds for me, or to any tradesmen on my account whatever.

Mr. Robinson knew that it would be useless to ask Mr. Harris's assistance–indeed his mind was too much depressed to make an exertion for the arrangement of his affairs. He was, therefore, after waiting three weeks in the custody of a sheriffs officer (during which time I had never left him for a single hour, day or night) obliged to submit to the necessity of becoming a captive.

For myself I cared but little; all my anxiety was for Mr. Robinson's repose and the health of my child. The apartment which we obtained was in the upper part of the building, overlooking a racket-ground. Mr. Robinson was expert in all exercises of strength or activity, and he found that amusement daily which I could not partake of. I had other occupations of a more interesting nature–the care of a beloved and still helpless daughter. [1]

During nine months and three weeks never once did I pass the threshold of our dreary habitation; though every allurement was offered, every effort was made, to draw me from my scene of domestic attachment. Numberless messages and letters from Lords Northington and Lyttelton, from Mr. Fitzgerald and many others, were conveyed to me. But they all, excepting Lord Northington's, were dictated in the language of gallantry, were replete with professions of *love* and wishes to release me from my unpleasant and humiliating situation–and were therefore treated with contempt, scorn, and indignation. For God can bear witness that, at that period, my mind had never entertained a thought of violating those vows which I had made to my husband at the altar.

What I suffered during this tedious captivity! My little volume of poems sold but indifferently; my health was considerably impaired; and the trifling income which Mr. Robinson received from his father was scarcely sufficient to support him. I will not enter into a tedious detail of vulgar sorrows, of vulgar scenes; I seldom quitted my apartment, and never till the evening, when for air and exercise I walked on the racket-ground with my husband.

It was during one of these night walks that my little daughter first blessed my ears with the articulation of words. The circumstance made a forcible and indelible impression on my mind. It was a clear moonlight evening; the infant was in the arms of her nursery maid; she was dancing her up and down, and was playing with her; her eyes were fixed on the moon, to which she pointed with her small forefinger. On a sudden a cloud passed over it, and the child, with a slow falling of her hand, articulately sighed, *"All gone"* This had been a customary expression with her maid, whenever the infant wanted anything which it was deemed prudent to withhold or to hide from her. These little nothings will appear insignificant to the common reader, but to the parent whose heart is ennobled by sensibility they will become matters of important interest. I can only add, that I walked till near midnight, watching every cloud that passed over the moon, and as often, with a rapturous sensation, hearing my little prattler repeat her observation.

Having much leisure and many melancholy hours, I again turned my thoughts towards the muses. I chose *Captivity* for the subject of my pen, and soon composed a quarto poem of some length; it was superior to my former productions; but it was full of defects, replete with weak or laboured lines. I never now read my early compositions without a suffusion on my cheek, which marks my humble opinion of them.

At this period I was informed that the Duchess of Devonshire [1] was the admirer and patroness of literature. With a mixture of timidity and hope I sent her Grace a neatly bound volume of my poems, accompanied by a short letter apologising for their defects, and pleading my age as the only excuse for their inaccuracy. My brother, who was a charming youth, was the bearer of my first literary offering at the shrine of nobility. The Duchess admitted him; and with the most generous and amiable sensibility inquired some particulars respecting my situation, with a request that on the following day I would make her a visit.

I knew not what to do. Her liberality claimed my compliance; yet, as I had never, during my husband's long captivity, quitted him for half an hour, I felt a sort of reluctance that pained the romantic firmness of my mind, while I meditated what I considered as a breach of my domestic attachment. However, at the particular and earnest request of Mr. Robinson, I consented, and accordingly accepted the Duchess's invitation.

During my seclusion from the world I had adapted my dress to my situation. Neatness was at all times my pride; but now plainness was the conformity to necessity. Simple habiliments became the abode of adversity; and the plain brown satin gown, which I wore on my first visit to the Duchess of Devonshire, appeared to me as strange as a birthday court-suit to a newly-married citizen's daughter.

To describe the Duchess's look and manner when she entered the back drawing-room of Devonshire House would be impracticable; mildness and sensibility beamed in her eyes and irradiated her countenance. She expressed her surprise at seeing so young a person, who had already experienced such vicissitude of fortune; she lamented that my destiny was so little proportioned to what she was pleased to term my desert, and with a tear of gentle sympathy requested that I would accept a proof of her good wishes. I had not words to express my feelings, and was departing, when the Duchess requested me to call on her very often, and to bring my little daughter with me.

Duchess of Devonshire
from an Engraving by Bartolozzi after Hamm

I made frequent visits to the amiable Duchess, and was at all times received with the warmest proofs of friendship. My little girl, to whom I was still a nurse, generally accompanied me, and always experienced the kindest caresses from my admired patroness, my liberal and affectionate friend. Frequently the Duchess inquired most minutely into the story of my sorrows, and as often gave me tears of the most spontaneous sympathy.

But such was my destiny, that while I cultivated the esteem of this best of women, by a conduct which was above the reach of reprobation, my husband, even though I was the partner of his captivity, the devoted slave to his necessities, indulged in the lowest and most degrading intrigues; frequently, during my short absence with the Duchess–for I never quitted the prison but to obey her summons–he was known to admit the most abandoned of their sex–women whose low licentious lives were such as to render them the shame and outcasts of society. These disgraceful meetings were arranged, even while I was in my own apartment, in a next room, and by the assistance of an Italian who was also there a captive. I was apprised of the proceeding, and I questioned Mr. Robinson upon the subject. He denied the charge; but I availed myself of an opportunity that offered, and was convinced that my husband's infidelities were both frequent and disgraceful.

Still I pursued my plan of the most rigid domestic propriety; still I preserved my faith inviolate, my name unsullied. At times I endured the most poignant sufferings, from the pain of disappointed hopes, and the pressure of pecuniary distresses.

During my long seclusion from society, for I could not associate with those whom destiny had placed in a similar predicament, not one of my female friends even inquired what was become of me. Those who had been protected and received with the most cordial hospitality by me in my more happy hours, now neglected all the kind condolence of sympathetic feeling, and shunned both me and my dreary habitation. From that hour I have never felt the affection for my own sex which perhaps some women feel; I have never taught my heart to cherish their friendship, or to depend on their attentions beyond the short perspective of a prosperous day. Indeed I have almost uniformly found my own sex my most inveterate enemies; I have experienced little kindness from them, though my bosom has often ached with the pang inflicted by their envy, slander, and malevolence.

The Italian whom I took occasion to mention as the *cicerone* of my husband's gallantries, was named Albanesi. He was the husband to a beautiful Roman woman of that name, who had some years before attracted considerable attention in the hemisphere of gallantry, where she had shone as a brilliant constellation. She had formerly been the mistress of a Prince de Courland, and afterwards of the Count de Belgeioso, the Imperial Ambassador; but at the period in which I first saw her she was, I believe, devoted to a life of unrestrained impropriety. She frequently came to visit her husband, who had held a situation in the opera-house during the management of Mr. Hobart, [1] now Earl of Buckinghamshire. I remember she was one of the handsomest women I had ever seen, and that her dress was the most extravagantly splendid. Satins, richly embroidered, or trimmed with point-lace, were her daily habiliments; and her personal attractions were considerably augmented by the peculiar dignity and grace with which she walked: in a few words, this woman was a striking sample of beauty and of profligacy.

Whenever she came to visit her *sposo* she never failed to obtrude herself on my seclusion. Mr. Robinson rather encouraged than shunned her visits, and I was obliged to receive the beautiful Angelina (for such was her Christian name), however repugnant such an associate was to my feelings. At every interview she took occasion to ridicule my romantic domestic attachment; laughed at my folly in wasting my youth (for I was not then eighteen years of age) in such a disgraceful obscurity; and pictured, in all the glow of fanciful scenery, the splendid life into which I might enter, if I would but know my own power, and break the fetters of matrimonial restriction. She once told me that she had mentioned to the Earl of Pembroke, that there was a young married lady in the most humiliating captivity with her husband; she said that she had described my person, and that Lord Pembroke was ready to offer me his services.

This proposal fully proclaimed the meaning of Signora Albanesi's visits, and I resolved in future to avoid all conversation with her. She was at that time between thirty and forty years of age, and her day of splendour was hourly sinking to the obscurity of neglect; she was nevertheless still reluctant to resign the dazzling meteors which fashion had scattered in her way, and, having sacrificed every personal feeling for the gratification of her vanity, she now sought to build a gaudy transient fabric on the destruction of another. In addition to her persuasions, her husband, Angelo Albanesi, constantly made the world of gallantry the subject of his conver- sation. Whole evenings has he sitten in our apartment telling long stories of intrigue, praising the liberality of one nobleman, the romantic chivalry of another, the sacrifice which a third had made to an adored object, and the splendid income which a fourth would bestow on any young lady of education and mental endowments who would accept his protection and be the partner of his fortune. I always smiled at Albanesi's innuendoes; and I still found some amusement in his society when he thought fit to divest his conversation of his favourite topic. This Italian, though neither young nor even tolerably well-looking, was uncommonly entertaining; he could sing, likewise imitate various musical instruments, was an excellent buffoon, and a very neat engraver; some of his plates were executed under the inspection of Sherwin, and he was considered as a very promising artist.

Were I to describe one-half of what I suffered during fifteen months' captivity, the world would consider it as the invention of a novel. But Mr. Robinson knows what I endured, and how patiently, how correctly I suited my mind to the strict propriety of wedded life; he knows that my duty as a wife was exemplary, my chastity inviolate; he knows that neither poverty nor obscurity, neither the tauntings of the world nor his neglect, could tempt me even to the smallest error; he knows that I bore my afflicting humiliations with a cheerful uncomplaining spirit; that I toiled honourably for his comfort; and that my attentions were exclusively dedicated to him and to my infant.

The period now arrived when Mr. Robinson, by setting aside some debts, and by giving fresh bonds and fresh securities for others, once more obtained his liberty. I immediately conveyed the intelligence to my lovely Duchess of Devonshire, and she wrote me a letter of kind congratulation: she was then at Chatsworth.

The first moments of emancipation were delightful to the senses. I felt as though I had been newly born; I longed to see all my old and intimate associates, and almost forgot that they had so unworthily neglected me. Everything that had passed now appeared like a melancholy vision. The gloom had dissolved, and a new perspective seemed to brighten before me.

The first place of public entertainment I went to was Vauxhall. I had frequently found occasion to observe a mournful contrast when I had quitted the elegant apartment of Devonshire House to enter the dark galleries of a prison; but the sensation which I felt on hearing the music and beholding the gay throng, during this first visit in public after so long a seclusion, was indescribable. During the evening we met many old acquaintances—some who pretended ignorance of our past embarrassments, and others who joined us with the ease of fashionable apathy; among these was Lord Lyttelton, who insolently remarked, "that, notwithstanding all that had passed, I was handsomer than ever." I made no reply, but by a look of scornful indignation, which silenced the bold, the unfeeling commentator, and convinced him that, though fallen in fortune, I was still high in pride.

Mr. Robinson having once more obtained his liberty, how were we to subsist honourably and above reproach? He applied to his father, but every aid was refused; he could not follow his profession, because he had not completed his articles of clerkship. I resolved on turning my thoughts towards literary labour, and projected a variety of works, by which I hoped to obtain at least a decent independence. Alas! How little did I then know either the fatigue or the hazard of mental occupations! How little did I foresee that the day would come when my health would be impaired, my thoughts perpetually employed, in so destructive a pursuit! At the moment that I write this page I feel in every fibre of my brain the fatal conviction that it is a *destroying labour*.

It was at this moment of anxiety, of hope, of fear, that my thoughts once more were turned to a dramatic life; and, walking with my husband in St. James's Park, late in the autumn, we were accosted by Mr. Brereton, of Drury Lane Theatre. I had not seen him during the last two years, and he seemed rejoiced in having met us. At that period we lodged at Lyne's, the confectioner, in Old Bond Street. Mr. Brereton went home and dined with us; and after dinner the conversation turned on my partiality to the stage, which he earnestly recommended as a scene of great promise to what he termed my promising talents. The idea rushed like electricity through my brain. I asked Mr. Robinson's opinion, and he now readily consented to my making the trial. He had repeatedly written to his father, requesting even the smallest aid towards our support until he could embark in his profession; but every letter remained unanswered, and we had no hope but in our own mental exertions.

Some time after this period we removed to a more quiet situation, and occupied a very neat and comfortable suite of apartments in Newman Street. I was then some months advanced in a state of domestic solicitude, and my health seemed in a precarious state, owing to my having too long devoted myself to the duties of a mother in nursing my eldest daughter Maria. It was in this lodging that, one morning, wholly unexpectedly, Mr. Brereton made us a second visit, bringing with him a friend, whom he introduced on entering the drawing-room. This stranger was Mr. Sheridan. [1]

I was overwhelmed with confusion. I know not why, but I felt a sense of mortification when I observed that my appearance was carelessly *dèshabille* , and my mind as little prepared for what I guessed to be the motive of his visit. I, however, soon recovered my recollection, and the theatre was consequently the topic of discourse.

At Mr. Sheridan's earnest entreaties I recited some passages from Shakespeare. I was alarmed and timid; but the gentleness of his manners, and the impressive encouragement he gave me, dissipated my fears and tempted me to go on.

Mr. Sheridan had then recently purchased a share of Drury Lane Theatre, in conjunction with Mr. Lacey and Dr. Ford; he was already celebrated as the author of The Rivals and The Duenna, and his mind was evidently portrayed in his manners, which were strikingly and bewitchingly attractive.

The encouragement which I received in this essay, and the praises which Mr. Sheridan lavishly bestowed, determined me to retake a public trial of my talents; and several visits, which were rapidly repeated by Mr. Sheridan, at length produced an arrangement for that period. My intention was intimated to Mr. Garrick, who, though he had for some seasons retired from the stage, kindly promised protection, and as kindly undertook to be my tutor.

The only objection which I felt to the idea of appearing on the stage was my then increasing state of domestic solicitude. I was, at the period when Mr. Sheridan was first presented to me, some months advanced in that situation which afterwards, by the birth of Sophia, made me a second time a mother. Yet such was my imprudent fondness for Maria, that I was still a nurse; and my constitution was very considerably impaired by the effects of these combined circumstances.

An appointment was made in the green-room of Drury Lane Theatre. Mr. Garrick, Mr. Sheridan, Mr. Brereton, and my husband were present; I there recited the principal scenes of Juliet (Mr. Brereton repeating those of Romeo), and Mr. Garrick, without hesitation, fixed on that character as the trial of my *dèbut*.

It is impossible to describe the various emotions of hope and fear that possessed my mind when the important day was announced in the play-bills. I wrote to the Duchess of Devonshire at Chatsworth, informing her of my purposed trial, and received a kind letter of approbation, sanctioning my plan and wishing me success. Every longing of my heart seemed now to be completely gratified; and, with zeal bordering on delight, I prepared for my approaching effort.

Mr. Garrick had been indefatigable at the rehearsals, frequently going through the whole character of Romeo himself until he was completely exhausted with the fatigue of recitation. This was only a short period before the death of that distinguished actor.

The theatre was crowded with fashionable spectators; the green-room and orchestra (where Mr. Garrick sat during the night) were thronged with critics. My dress was a pale pink satin, trimmed with crape, richly spangled with silver; my head was ornamented with white feathers, and my monumental suit, for the last scene, was white satin and completely plain, excepting that I wore a veil of the most transparent gauze, which fell quite to my feet from the back of my head, and a string of beads round my waist, to which was suspended a cross appropriately fashioned.

When I approached the side wing my heart throbbed convulsively; I then began to fear that my resolution would fail, and I leaned upon the Nurse's arm, almost fainting. Mr. Sheridan and several other friends encouraged me to proceed; and at length, with trembling limbs and fearful apprehension, I approached the audience.

The thundering applause that greeted me nearly overpowered all my faculties. I stood mute and bending with alarm, which did not subside till I had feebly articulated the few sentences of the first short scene, during the whole of which I had never once ventured to look at the audience.

On my return to the green-room I was again encouraged, as far as my looks were deemed deserving of approbation; for of my powers nothing yet could be known, my fears having as it were palsied both my voice and action. The second scene being the masquerade, I had time to collect myself. I never shall forget the sensation which rushed through my bosom when I first looked towards the pit. I beheld a gradual ascent of heads. All eyes were fixed upon me, and the sensation they conveyed was awfully impressive; but the keen, the penetrating eyes of Mr. Garrick, darting their lustre from the centre of the orchestra, were, beyond all others, the objects most conspicuous. [1]

As I acquired courage, I found the applause augment; and the night was concluded with peals of clamorous approbation. I was complimented on all sides; but the praise of one object, whom most I wished to please, was flattering even to the extent of human vanity. I then experienced, for the first time in my life, a gratification which language could not utter. I heard one of the most fascinating men, and the most distinguished geniuses of the age, honour me with partial approbation. A new sensation seemed to awake in my bosom; I felt that emulation which the soul delights to encourage, where the attainment of fame will be pleasing to the esteemed object. I had till that period known no impulse beyond that of friendship; I had been an example of conjugal fidelity; but I had never known the perils to which the feeling heart is subjected in a union of regard wholly uninfluenced by the affections of the soul.

The second character which I played was Amanda, in A Trip to Scarborough. [1] The play was altered from Vanbrugh's Relapse; and the audience, supposing it was a new piece, on finding themselves deceived, expressed a considerable degree of disapprobation. I was terrified beyond imagination when Mrs. Yates, no longer able to bear the hissing of the audience, quitted the scene, and left me alone to encounter the critic tempest. I stood for some moments as though I had been petrified. Mr. Sheridan, from the side wing, desired me not to quit the boards; the late Duke of Cumberland,[2] from the stage box, bade me take courage: "It is not you, but the play, they hiss," said his Royal Highness. I curtsied; and that curtsey seemed to electrify the whole house, for a thundering appeal of encouraging applause followed. The comedy was suffered to go on, and is to this hour a stock play at Drury Lane Theatre.

The third character I played was Statira, in Alexander the Great. Mr. Lacey, then one of the proprietors of Drury Lane Theatre, was the hero of the night, and the part of Roxana was performed by Mrs. Melmoth. Again I was received with an *éclat* that gratified my vanity. My dress was white and blue, made after the Persian costume; and though it was then singular on the stage, I wore neither a hoop nor powder; my feet were bound by sandals richly ornamented, and the whole dress was picturesque and characteristic.

Though I was always received with the most flattering approbation, the characters in which I was most popular were Ophelia, Juliet, and Rosalind. Palmira was also one of my most approved representations. The last character which I played was Sir Harry Revel, in Lady Craven's comedy of The Miniature Picture; and the epilogue song in The Irish Widow[1] was my last farewell to the labour of my profession.

Mr. Sheridan now informed me he wished that I would accustom myself to appear in comedy, because tragedy seemed evidently, as well as my *forte*, to be my preference. At the same time he acquainted me that he wished me to perform a part in The School for Scandal. I was now so unshaped by my increasing size that I made my excuses, informing Mr. Sheridan that probably I should be confined to my chamber at the period when his since celebrated play would first make its appearance. He accepted the apology, and in a short time I gave to the world my second child, Sophia. I now resided in Southampton Street, Covent Garden.

Previous to this event I had my benefit night, on which I performed the part of Fanny in The Clandestine Marriage. Mr. King, the Lord Ogleby; Miss Pope, Miss Sterling; and Mrs. Heidelberg, Mrs. Hopkins.

Mr. Sheridan's attentions to me were unremitting. He took pleasure in promoting my consequence at the theatre; he praised my talents, and he interested himself in my domestic comforts. I was engaged previous to my *début* and I received what at that time was considered as a handsome salary. My benefit was flatteringly attended. The boxes were filled with persons of the very highest rank and fashion, and I looked forward with delight both to celebrity and to fortune.

At the end of six weeks I lost my infant. She expired in my arms in convulsions, and my distress was indescribable. On the day of its dissolution Mr. Sheridan called on me; the little sufferer was on my lap, and I was watching it with agonising anxiety. Five months had then elapsed since Mr. Sheridan was first introduced to me; and though, during that period, I had seen many proofs of his exquisite sensibility, I never had witnessed one which so strongly impressed my mind as his countenance on entering my apartment. Probably he has forgotten the feeling of the moment, but its impression will by me be remembered for ever.

I had not power to speak. All he uttered was, "Beautiful little creature!" at the same time looking on my infant, and sighing with a degree of sympathetic sorrow which penetrated my soul. Had I ever heard *such a sigh* from a husband's bosom? Alas! I never knew the sweet soothing solace of wedded sympathy; I never was beloved by him whom destiny allotted to be the legal ruler of my actions. I do not condemn Mr. Robinson; I but too well know that we cannot command our affections. I only lament that he did not observe some decency in his infidelities; and that while he gratified his own caprice, he forgot how much he exposed his *wife* to the most degrading mortifications.

The death of Sophia so deeply affected my spirits that I was rendered totally incapable of appearing again that season. I therefore obtained Mr. Sheridan's permission to visit *Bristol* Bath for the recovery of my repose. From Bath I went to Bristol–to *Bristol!* Why does my pen seem suddenly arrested while I write the word? I know not why, but an undefinable melancholy always follows the idea of my native birthplace. I instantly beheld the Gothic structure, the lonely cloisters, the lofty aisles, of the antique minster–for, within a few short paces of its walls, this breast, which has never known, *one year of happiness*, first palpitated on inhaling the air of this bad world! Is it within its consecrated precincts that this heart shall shortly moulder? Heaven only knows, and to its will I bow implicitly.

I transcribe this passage on the 29th of March, 1800. I feel my health decaying, my spirit broken. I look back without regret that so many of my days are numbered; and, were it in my power to choose, I would not wish to measure them again. But whither am I wandering? I will resume my melancholy story.

Still restless, still perplexed with painful solicitudes, I returned to London. I had not then, by many months, completed my nineteenth year. On my arrival I took lodgings in Leicester Square. Mr. Sheridan came to see me on my return to town, and communicated the melancholy fate of Mr. Thomas Linley,[1] the late brother of Mrs. Sheridan–he was unfortunately drowned at the Duke of Ancaster's. In a few days after, Mr. Sheridan again made me a visit, with a proposal for an engagement to play during the summer at Mr. Colman's theatre in the Haymarket.[2] I had refused several offers from provincial managers, and felt an almost insurmountable aversion to the idea of strolling. Mr. Sheridan nevertheless strongly recommended me to the acceptance of Mr. Colman's offer; and I at last agreed to it, upon condition that the characters I should be expected to perform were selected and limited. To this Mr. Colman readily consented.

The first part which was placed in the list was Nancy Lovel, in the comedy of The Suicide. I received the written character, and waited the rehearsal; but my astonishment was infinite when I saw the name of Miss Farren [1] announced in the bills. I wrote a letter to Mr. Coleman, requesting an explanation. He replied that he had promised the part to Miss Farren, who had then performed one or two seasons at the Haymarket Theatre. I felt myself insulted. I insisted on Mr. Colman fulfilling his engagement, or on giving me liberty to quit London: the latter he refused. I demanded to perform the part of Nancy Lovel. Mr. Colman was too partial to Miss Farren to hazard offending her. I refused to play till I had this first character, as by agreement, restored to me, and the summer passed without my once performing, though my salary was paid weekly and regularly.

During the following winter I performed, with increasing approbation, the following characters:–

Ophelia, in Hamlet.
Viola, in Twelfth Night.
Jacintha, in The Suspicious Husband.
Fidelia, in The Plain Dealer.
Rosalind, in As You Like It.
Oriana, in The Inconstant.
Octavia, in All for Love.
Perdita, in The Winter's Tale.
Palmira, in Mahomet.
Cordelia, in King Lear.
Alinda, in The Law of Lombardy.
The Irish Widow.
Araminta, in The Old Bachelor.
Sir Harry Revel, in The Miniature Picture.
Emily, in The Runaway.
Miss Richley, in The Discovery.
Statira, in Alexander the Great.
Juliet, in Romeo and Juliet.
Amanda, in The Trip to Scarborough.
Lady Anne, in Richard the Third.
Imogen, in Cymbeline.
Lady Macbeth, [1] in Macbeth, &c., &c.

It was now that I began to know the perils attendant on a dramatic life. It was at this period that the most alluring temptations were held out to alienate me from the paths of domestic quiet–domestic happiness I cannot say, for it never was my destiny to know it. But I had still the consolation of an unsullied name. I had the highest female patronage, a circle of the most respectable and partial friends.

Miss Farren
from an Engraving by Knight after Lawrence

During this period I was daily visited by my best of mothers. My youngest brother had, the preceding winter, departed for Leghorn, where my eldest had been many years established as a merchant of the first respectability.

Were I to mention the names of those who held forth the temptations of fortune at this moment of public peril, I might create some reproaches in many families of the fashionable world. Among others who offered most liberally to purchase my indiscretion was the late Duke of Rutland; a settlement of six hundred pounds per annum was proposed as the means of estranging me entirely from my husband. I refused the offer. I wished to remain, in the eyes of the public, deserving of its patronage. I shall not enter into a minute detail of temptations which assailed my fortitude.

The flattering and zealous attentions which Mr. Sheridan evinced were strikingly contrasting with the marked and increasing neglect of my husband. I now found that he supported two women, in one house, in Maiden Lane, Covent Garden. The one was a figure-dancer in Drury Lane Theatre; the other, a woman of professed libertinism. With these he passed all his hours that he could steal from me; and I found that my salary was at times inadequate to the expenses which were incurred by an enlarged circle of new acquaintance, which Mr. Robinson had formed since my appearance in the dramatic scene. Added to this, the bond creditors became so clamorous, that the whole of my benefits were appropriated to their demands; and on the second year after my appearance at Drury Lane Theatre, Mr. Robinson once more persuaded me to make a visit at Tregunter.

I was now received with more civility, and more warmly welcomed, than I had been on any former arrival. Though the *assumed sanctity* of Miss Robinson's manners condemned a dramatic life, the labour was deemed *profitable* and the supposed immorality was consequently *tolerated* However repugnant to my feelings this visit was, still I hoped that it would promote my husband's interest, and confirm his reconciliation to his father; I therefore resolved on undertaking it. I now felt that I could support myself honourably; and the consciousness of independence is the only true felicity in this world of humiliations.

Mr. Harris was now established in Tregunter House, and several parties were formed, both at home and abroad, for my amusement. I was consulted as the very oracle of fashions; I was gazed at and examined with the most inquisitive curiosity. Mrs. Robinson, the promising young actress, was a very different personage from Mrs. Robinson who had been overwhelmed with sorrows, and came to ask an asylum under the roof of vulgar ostentation. I remained only a fortnight in Wales, and then returned to London, to prepare for the opening of the theatre.

We stopped at Bath on our way to town, where Mr. Robinson met with Mr. George Brereton, with whom, at Newmarket, he had some time before become acquainted. Mr. Brereton was a man of fortune and married to his beautiful cousin, the daughter of Major Brereton, then master of the ceremonies at Bath. At a former period Mr. Robinson had owed a sum of money to Mr. George Brereton, for which he had given a promissory note. On our arrival at Bath we received a visit from this creditor, who assured Mr. Robinson that he was in no haste for the payment of his note, and at the same time very earnestly pressed us to remain a few days in that fashionable city. We were in no hurry to return to London, having still more than three weeks' holidays. We resided at the "Three Tuns," one of the best inns, and Mr. Brereton was on all occasions particularly attentive.

The motive of this assiduity was at length revealed to me, by a violent and fervent declaration of love, which astonished and perplexed me. I knew that Mr. Brereton was of a most impetuous temper; that he had fought many duels; that he was capable of any outrage; and that he had my husband completely in his power. Every advance which he had the temerity to make was by me rejected with indignation. I had not resolution to inform Mr. Robinson of his danger, and I thought that the only chance of escaping it was to set out immediately for Bristol, where I wished to pass a few days, previous to my return to the metropolis.

On the following morning, as we were quitting the inn in Temple Street, to visit Clifton, Mr. Robinson was arrested at the suit of Mr. George Brereton, who waited himself in an upper room in order to see the writ executed. I forget the exact sum for which Mr. Robinson had given his promissory note, but I well remember that it was in magnitude beyond his power to pay. Our consternation was indescribable.

In a few minutes after I was informed that a lady wished to speak with me. Concluding that it was some old acquaintance, and happy to feel that in this perplexing dilemma I had still a friend to speak to, I followed the waiter into another room. Mr. Robinson was detained by the sheriffs officer.

On entering the apartment I beheld Mr. Brereton.

"Well, madam," said he, with a sarcastic smile, "you have involved your husband in a pretty embarrassment! Had you not been severe towards me, not only this paltry debt would have been cancelled, but any sum that I could command would have been at his service. He has now either to pay me, to fight me, or to go to a prison; and all because you treat me with such unexampled rigour."

I entreated him to reflect before he drove me to distraction.

"I have reflected," said he, "and I find that you possess the power to do with me what you will. Promise to return to Bath–to behave more kindly–and I will this moment discharge your husband."

I burst into tears.

"You cannot be so inhuman as to propose such terms!" said I.

"The inhumanity is on your side," answered Mr. Brereton. "But I have no time to lose; I must return to Bath; my wife is dangerously ill; and I do not wish to have my name exposed in a business of this nature."

"Then for Heaven's sake release my hus- band!" said I. Mr. Brereton smiled as he rang the bell, and ordered the waiter to look for his carriage. I now lost all command of myself, and, with the most severe invective, condemned the infamy of his conduct. "I *will* return to Bath," said I; "but it shall be to expose *your* dishonourable, your barbarous machinations. I will inform that lovely wife how treacherously you have acted. I will proclaim to the world that the common arts of seduction are not sufficiently depraved for the mind of a libertine and a gamester,"

I uttered these words in so loud a tone of voice that he changed colour, and desired me to be discreet and patient.

"Never while you insult me, and hold my husband in your power," said I. "You have carried outrage almost to its fullest extent; you have awakened all the pride and all the resentment of my soul, and I will proceed as I think proper."

He now endeavoured to soothe me. He assured me that he was actuated by a sincere regard for me; and that, knowing how little my husband valued me, he thought it would be an act of kindness to estrange me from him. "His neglect of you will justify any step you may take," added he; "and it is a matter of universal astonishment that you, who upon other occasions can act with such becoming spirit, should tamely continue to bear such infidelities from a husband." I shuddered; for this plea had, in many instances, been urged as an excuse for libertine advances; and the indifference with which I was treated was, in the theatre, and in all my circle of friends, a subject of conversation.

Distressed beyond the power of utterance at this new humiliation, I paced the room with agonising inquietude.

"How little does such a husband deserve such a wife!" continued Mr. Brereton; "how tasteless must he be, to leave such a woman for the very lowest and most degraded of the sex! Quit him, and fly with me. I am ready to make any sacrifice you demand. Shall I propose to Mr. Robinson to let you go? Shall I offer him his liberty on condition that he allows you to separate yourself from him? By his conduct he proves that he does not love you; why then labour to support him?"

I was almost frantic.

"Here, madam," continued Mr. Brereton, after pausing four or five minutes—"here is your husband's release." So saying, he threw a written paper on the table. "Now," added he, "I rely on your generosity."

I trembled, and was incapable of speaking. Mr. Brereton conjured me to compose my spirits, and to conceal my distress from the people of the inn. "I will return to Bath," said he. "I shall there expect to see you." He now quitted the room. I saw him get into his chaise and drive from the inn door. I then hastened to my husband with the discharge; and all expenses of the arrest being shortly after settled, we set out for Bath.

Mr. Robinson scarcely inquired what had passed; but I assured him that my persuasions had produced so sudden a change in Mr. Brereton's conduct. I said that I hoped he would never again place his freedom in the hands of a gamester, or his wife's repose in the power of a libertine. He seemed insensible of the peril attending both the one and the other.

Expecting letters by the post, we waited the following day, which was Sunday, at Bath; though, in order to avoid Mr. Brereton, we removed to the White Lion Inn. But what was my astonishment, in the afternoon, when, standing at the window, I saw Mr. George Brereton walking on the opposite side of the way, with his wife and her no less lovely sister! I now found that the story of her dangerous illness was untrue, and I flattered myself that I was not seen before I retired from the window.

We now sat down to dinner, and in a few minutes Mr. George Brereton was announced by the waiter. He coldly bowed to me, and instantly made a thousand apologies to Mr. Robinson; declared that he had paid the note away; that he was menaced for the money and that he came to Bristol, though too late, to prevent the arrest which had happened. Mr. Robinson sceptically replied that it was now of little importance; and Mr. Brereton took his leave, saying that he should have the honour of seeing us again in the evening. We did not wait for his company, but immediately after dinner set out for London.

On my arrival in town I saw Mr. Sheridan, whose manner had lost nothing of its interesting attention. He continued to visit me very frequently, and always gave me the most friendly counsel.

He knew that I was not properly protected by Mr. Robinson, but he was too generous to build his gratification on the detraction of another. The happiest moments I then knew were passed in the society of this distinguished being. He saw me ill-bestowed upon a man who neither loved nor valued me; he lamented my destiny, but with such delicate propriety that it consoled while it revealed to me the unhappiness of my situation. On my return to town the Duke of Rutland renewed his solicitations. I also received the most unbounded professions of esteem and admiration from several other persons. Among the list, I was addressed with proposals of libertine nature by a *royal* duke, a *lofty* marquis, and a city merchant of considerable fortune, conveyed through the medium of milliners, mantua-makers, &c., &c. Just at this period my eldest brother visited England; but such was his unconquerable aversion to my profession as an actress, that he only once, during a residence of some months in London, attempted to see me perform. He then only attempted it; for, on my advancing on the boards, he started from his seat in the stage-box, and instantly quitted the theatre. My dear mother had no less a dislike to the pursuit: she never beheld me on the stage but with a painful regret. Fortunately my father remained some years out of England, so that he never saw me in my professional character.

My popularity increasing every night that I appeared, my prospects, both of fame and affluence, began to brighten. We now hired the house which is situated between the Hummums and the Bedford Arms, in Covent Garden; it had been built (I believe) by Dr. Fisher, who married the widow of the celebrated actor Powel; but Mr. Robinson took the premises of Mrs. Mattocks, of Covent Garden Theatre. The house was particularly convenient in every respect; but, above all, on account of its vicinity to Drury Lane. Here I hoped to enjoy, at least, some cheerful days, as I found that my circle of friends increased almost hourly.

One of those who paid me most attention was Sir John Lade. The good-natured baronet, who was then just of age, was our constant visitor, and cards contributed to beguile those evenings that were not devoted to dramatic labour. Mr. Robinson played more deeply than was discreet, but he was, at the end of a few weeks, a very considerable winner.

In proportion as play obtained its influence over my husband's mind, his small portion of remaining regard for me visibly decayed. We now had horses, a phaeton and ponies; and my fashions in dress were followed with flattering avidity. My house was thronged with visitors, and my morning *levèes* were crowded so that I could scarcely find a quiet hour for study. My brother by this time had returned to Italy.

Mr. Sheridan was still my most esteemed of friends. He advised me with the gentlest anxiety, and he warned me of the danger which expense would produce, and which might interrupt the rising progress of my dramatic reputation. He saw the trophies which flattery strewed in my way; and he lamented that I was on every side surrounded with temptations. There was a something beautifully sympathetic in every word he uttered; his admonitions seemed as if dictated by a prescient power, which told him that I was *destined to be deceived*

Situated as I was at this time, the effort was difficult to avoid the society of Mr. Sheridan. He was manager of the theatre. I could not avoid seeing and conversing with him at rehearsals and behind the scenes, and his conversation was always such as to fascinate and charm me. The brilliant reputation which he had justly acquired for superior talents, and the fame which was completed by his celebrated School for Scandal, had now rendered him so admired, that all ranks of people courted his society. The green-room was frequented by nobility and men of genius; among these were Mr. Fox [1] and the Earl of Derby. The stage was now enlightened by the very best critics, and embellished by the very highest talents; and it is not a little remarkable, that the drama was uncommonly productive, the theatre more than usually attended, during that season when the principal dramatic characters were performed by women under the age of twenty. Among these were Miss Farren (now Lady

Derby), Miss Walpole (now Mrs. Atkins), Miss P. Hopkins (now Mrs. John Kemble), and myself.

I had then been married more than four years; my daughter Maria Elizabeth was nearly three years old. I had been then seen and known at all public places from the age of fifteen; yet I knew as little of the world's deceptions as though I had been educated in the deserts of Siberia. I believed every woman friendly, every man sincere, till I discovered proofs that their characters were deceptive.

I had now performed two seasons, in tragedy and comedy, with Miss Farren and the late Mr. Henderson. My first appearance in Palmira (in Mahomet) was with the Zaphna of Mr. J. Bannister, the preceding year; and though the extraordinary comic powers of this excellent actor and amiable man have established his reputation as a comedian, his first essay in tragedy was considered as a night of the most distinguished promise. The Duchess of Devonshire still honoured me with her patronage and friendship, and I also possessed the esteem of several respectable and distinguished females.

The play of The Winter's Tale was this season commanded by their Majesties. [1] I never had performed before the royal family; and the first character in which I was destined to appear was that of Perdita. I had frequently played the part, both with the Hermione of Mrs. Hartley and of Miss Farren: but I felt a strange degree of alarm when I found my name announced to perform it before the royal family. [1]

In the green-room I was rallied on the occasion; and Mr. Smith, [2]whose gentlemanly manners and enlightened conversation rendered him an ornament to the profession, who performed the part of Leontes, laughingly exclaimed, "By Jove, Mrs. Robinson, you will make a conquest of the Prince; for tonight you look handsomer than ever." I smiled at the unmerited compliment, and little foresaw the vast variety of events that would arise from that night's exhibition!

As I stood in the wing opposite the Prince's box, waiting to go on the stage, Mr. Ford, the manager's son, and now a respectable defender of the laws, presented a friend who accompanied him; this friend was Lord Viscount Maiden, now Earl of Essex. [3]

We entered into conversation during a few minutes, the Prince of Wales all the time observing us, and frequently speaking to Colonel (now *General*) Lake, and to the Honourable Mr. Legge, brother to Lord Lewisham, who was in waiting on his Royal Highness. I hurried through the first scene, not without much embarrassment, owing to the fixed attention with which the Prince of Wales honoured me. Indeed, some flattering remarks which were made by his Royal Highness met my ear as I stood near his box, and I was overwhelmed with confusion.

The Prince's particular attention was observed by every one, and I was again rallied at the end of the play. On the last curtsy, the royal family condescendingly returned a bow to the performers; but just as the curtain was falling, my eyes met those of the Prince of Wales; and with a look that *I never shall forget* he gently inclined his head a second time; I felt the compliment, and blushed my gratitude.

During the entertainment Lord Malden never ceased conversing with me: he was young, pleasing, and perfectly accomplished. He remarked the particular applause which the Prince had bestowed on my performance; said a thousand civil things; and detained me in conversation till the evening's performance was concluded.

I was now going to my chair, which waited, when I met the royal family crossing the stage. I was again honoured with a very marked and low bow from the Prince of Wales. On my return home, I had a party to supper; and the whole conversation centred in encomiums on the person, graces, and amiable manners of the illustrious Heir-apparent.

Within two or three days of this time, Lord Malden made me a morning visit. Mr. Robinson was not at home, and I received him rather awkwardly. But his lordship's embarrassment far exceeded mine. He attempted to speak–paused, hesitated, apologised; I knew not why. He hoped I would pardon him; that I would not mention something he had to communicate; that I would consider the peculiar delicacy of his situation, and then act as I thought proper. I could not comprehend his meaning, and therefore requested that he would be explicit.

After some moments of evident rumination, he tremblingly drew a small letter from his pocket. I took it, and knew not what to say. It was addressed to PERDITA. I smiled, I believe rather sarcastically, and opened the *billet* It contained only a few words, but those expressive of more than common civility; they were signed FLORIZEL. [1]

"Well, my lord, and what does this mean? " said I, half angry.

"Can you not guess the writer? " said Lord Malden.

"Perhaps yourself, my lord," cried I, gravely.

"Upon my honour, no," said the Viscount. "I should not have dared so to address you on so short an acquaintance."

I pressed him to tell me from whom the letter came. He again hesitated; he seemed confused, and sorry that he had undertaken to deliver it.

"I hope that I shall not forfeit your good opinion," said he; " but–"

"But what, my lord? "

"I could not refuse–for the letter is from the Prince of Wales."

I was astonished; I confess that I was agi- tated; but I was also somewhat sceptical as to the truth of Lord Malden's assertion. I returned a formal and a doubtful answer, and his lordship shortly after took his leave.

A thousand times did I read this short but expressive letter. Still I did not implicitly believe that it was written by the Prince; I rather considered it as an experiment made by Lord Malden, either on my vanity or propriety of conduct. On the next evening the Viscount repeated his visit. We had a card-party of six or seven, and the Prince of Wales was again the subject of unbounded panegyric. Lord Malden spoke of his royal Highness's manners as the most polished and fascinating; of his temper as the most engaging; and of his mind, the most replete with every amiable sentiment. I heard these praises and my heart beat with conscious pride, while memory turned to the partial but delicately respectful letter which I had received on the preceding morning.

The next day Lord Malden brought me a second letter. He assured me that the Prince was most unhappy lest I should be offended at his conduct, and that he conjured me to go that night to the Oratorio, [1] where he would by some signal convince me that he was the writer of the letters, supposing I was still sceptical as to their authenticity.

I went to the Oratorio; and, on taking my seat in the balcony-box, the Prince almost instantaneously observed me. He held the printed bill before his face, and drew his hand across his forehead, still fixing his eyes on me. I was confused, and knew not what to do. My husband was with me, and I was fearful of his observing what passed. Still the Prince continued to make signs, such as moving his hand on the edge of the box as if writing, then speaking to the Duke of York [1] (then Bishop of Osnaburg), who also looked towards me with particular attention.

I now observed one of the gentlemen in waiting bring the Prince a glass of water; before he raised it to his lips he looked at me. So marked was his Royal Highness's conduct that many of the audience observed it; several persons in the pit directed their gaze at the place where I sat; and, on the following day, one of the diurnal prints observed that there was one passage in Dryden's Ode which seemed particularly interesting to the Prince of Wales, who–

> "Gazed on the fair
> Who caused his care,
> And sigh'd, and look'd, and sigh'd again." [1]

However flattering it might have been to female vanity to know that the most admired and most accomplished Prince in Europe was devotedly attached to me; however dangerous to the heart such idolatry as his Royal Highness, during many months, professed in almost daily letters, which were conveyed to me by Lord Malden, still I declined any interview with his Royal Highness. I was not insensible to all his powers of attraction; I thought him one of the most amiable of men. There was a beautiful ingenuousness in his language, a warm and enthusiastic adoration, expressed in every letter, which interested and charmed me. During the whole spring, till the theatre closed, this correspondence continued, every day giving me some new assurance of inviolable affection.

After we had corresponded some months without ever speaking to each other (for I still declined meeting his Royal Highness, from a dread of the *èclat* which such a connection would produce, and the fear of injuring him in the opinion of his royal relatives), I received, through the hands of Lord Malden, the Prince's portrait in miniature, painted by the late Mr. Meyer. This picture is now in my possession. Within the case was a small heart cut in paper, which I also have; on one side was written, *Je ne change qu'en mourant* On the other, *Unalterable to my perdita through life.*

During many months of confidential correspondence, I always offered his Royal Highness the best advice in my power; I disclaimed every sordid and interested thought; I recommended him to be patient till he should become his own master; to wait till he knew more of my mind and manners, before he engaged in a public attachment to me; and, above all, to do nothing that might incur the displeasure of his Royal Highness's family. I entreated him to recollect that he was young, and led on by the impetuosity of passion; that should I consent to quit my profession and my husband, I should be thrown entirely on his mercy. I strongly pictured the temptations to which beauty would expose him; the many arts that would be practised to undermine me in his affections; the public abuse which calumny and envy would heap upon me; and the misery I should suffer, if, after I had given him every proof of confidence, he should change in his sentiments towards me. To all this I received repeated assurances of inviolable affection; and I most firmly believe that his Royal Highness meant what he professed—indeed, his soul was too ingenuous, his mind too liberal, and his heart too susceptible, to deceive premeditatedly, or to harbour even for a moment the idea of deliberate deception.

Florizel. *Perdita.*

At every interview with Lord Malden I perceived that he regretted the task he had undertaken; but he assured me that the Prince was almost frantic whenever he suggested a wish to decline interfering. Once I remember his lordship's telling me that the late Duke of Cumberland had made him a visit early in the morning, at his house in Clarges Street, informing him that the

Prince was most wretched on my account, and imploring him to continue his services only a short time longer. The Prince's establishment was then in agitation: at this period his Royal Highness still resided in Buckingham House.

A proposal was now made that I should meet his Royal Highness at his apartments, in the disguise of male attire. I was accustomed to perform in that dress, and the Prince had seen me, I believe, in the character of the Irish Widow. To this plan I decidedly objected. The indelicacy of such a step, as well as the danger of detection, made me shrink from the proposal. My refusal threw his Royal Highness into the most distressing agitation, as was expressed by the letter which I received on the following morning. Lord Malden again lamented that he had engaged himself in the intercourse, and declared that he had himself conceived so violent a passion for me that he was the most miserable and unfortunate of mortals.

During this period, though Mr. Robinson was a stranger to my epistolary intercourse with the Prince, his conduct was entirely neglectful. He was perfectly careless respecting my fame and my repose; passed his leisure hours with the most abandoned women, and even my own servants complained of his illicit advances. I remember one, who was plain even to ugliness; she was short, ill-made, squalid, and dirty; once, on my return from a rehearsal, I found that this woman was locked with my husband in my chamber. I also knew that Mr. Robinson continued his connection with a female who lodged in Maiden Lane, and who was only one of the few that proved his domestic apostacy.

His indifference naturally produced an alienation of esteem on my side, and the increasing adoration of the most enchanting of mortals hourly reconciled my mind to the idea of a separation. The unbounded assurances of lasting affection which I received from his Royal Highness in many scores of the most eloquent letters, the contempt which I experi- enced from my husband, and the perpetual labour which I underwent for his support, at length began to weary my fortitude. Still I was reluctant to become the theme of public animadversion, and still I remonstrated with my husband on the unkindness of his conduct.

The narrative of Mrs. Robinson closes here.

CONTINUATION.

BY A FRIEND.

AMONG those persons who have at various periods attracted the attention of the public, there are few whose virtues have been so little known, or whose characters have been so unfairly estimated, as the subject of the preceding memoir. To compress within narrow limits the numerous circumstances by which the later years of Mrs. Robinson's life were chequered, will be a task of no little difficulty. The earlier periods of her existence, rendered more interesting as narrated by her own pen, have doubtlessly been justly appreciated by the reflecting and candid reader, whose sympathy they could not fail to awaken. That she lived not to conclude the history of a life scarcely less eventful than unfortunate, cannot but afford a subject of sincere regret.

The conflicts which shook the mind, and the passions which succeeded to each other in the breast of Mrs. Robinson, at the period when her narrative closes, a crisis perhaps the most important in her life, may be more easily conceived than described. A laborious though captivating profession, the profits of which were unequal to the expenses of her establishment, and the assiduities of her illustrious lover, to whom she naturally looked for protection, combined to divide her attention and bewilder her inexperienced mind. The partiality of her royal admirer had begun to excite observation, to awaken curiosity, and to provoke the malignant passions which, under an affected concern for decorum, assumed the guise of virtue. The daily prints teemed with hints of the favour of Mrs. Robinson with "one whose manners were resistless, and whose smile was victory." These circumstances, added to the constant devoirs of Lord Malden, whose attentions were as little understood as maliciously interpreted, conspired to distract a young creature, whose exposed situation, whose wavering and unformed character, rendered her but too obnoxious to a thousand errors and perils.

To terminate her correspondence with the Prince appeared the most painful remedy that could be adopted by a heart fascinated with his accomplishments and soothed by his professions of inviolable attachment. She was aware that, in the eye of the world, the reputation of the wife is supposed unsullied while the husband, enduring passively his dishonour, gives to her the sanction of his protection. The circles of fashion afforded more than one instance of this obliging acquiescence in matrimonial turpitude. Could Mrs. Robinson have reconciled it to her own feelings to remain under the roof of her husband, whose protection she had forfeited, and to add insult to infidelity, the attentions of her illustrious admirer might have given to her popularity an additional *éclat*. Neither might her husband have suffered in his worldly prospects, from being to the motives of his royal visitor a little complaisantly blind. But her ingenuous nature would not permit her to render the man for whom she had once felt an affection an object of ridicule and contempt. She determined therefore to brave the world, and, for a support against its censures, to rely on the protection and friendship of him to whom she sacrificed its respect.

The managers of Drury Lane Theatre, suspect- ing that Mrs. Robinson purposed, at the conclusion of the season, to withdraw from the stage, omitted no means that might tend to induce her to renew her engagements. With this view, they offered a considerable advance to her salary, while to their solicitations she returned undecisive answers. Hourly rising in a profession to which she was enthusiastically attached, the public plaudits which her appearance never failed to excite, were too gratifying to be relinquished without regret.

During this irresolution, she was persecuted by numerous anonymous letters, which she continued to treat with derision or contempt. The correspondence between Mrs. Robinson and the Prince had hitherto been merely epistolary. This intercourse had lasted several months, Mrs. Robinson not having acquired sufficient courage to venture a personal interview, and bid defiance to the reproaches of the world.

At length, after many alternations of feeling, an interview with her royal lover was consented to by Mrs. Robinson, and proposed, by the management of Lord Malden, to take place at his lordship's residence in Dean Street, Mayfair. But the restricted situation of the prince, controlled by a rigid tutor, rendered this project of difficult execution. A visit to Buckingham House was then mentioned; to which Mrs. Robinson positively objected, as a rash attempt, abounding in peril to her august admirer. Lord Malden being again consulted, it was determined that the Prince should meet Mrs. Robinson for a few moments at Kew, [1] on the banks of the Thames, opposite to the old palace, then the summer residence of the elder princes. For an account of this incident, an extract from a letter of Mrs. Robinson, written some years afterwards to a valued and since deceased friend, who during the period of these events resided in America, may not be unacceptable to the reader. The date of this letter is in 1783.

"At length an evening was fixed for this long-dreaded interview. Lord Malden and myself dined at the inn on the island between Kew and Brentford. We waited the signal for crossing the river in a boat which had been engaged for the purpose. Heaven can witness how many conflicts my agitated heart endured at this most important moment! I admired the Prince; I felt grateful for his affection. He was the most engaging of created beings. I had corresponded with him during many months, and his eloquent letters, the exquisite sensibility which breathed through every line, his ardent professions of adoration, had combined to shake my feeble resolution. The handkerchief was waved on the opposite shore; but the signal was, by the dusk of the evening, rendered almost imperceptible. Lord Malden took my hand, I stepped into the boat, and in a few minutes we landed before the iron gates of old Kew Palace. The interview was but of a moment. The Prince of Wales and the Duke of York (then Bishop of Osnaburg) were walking down the avenue. They hastened to meet us. A few words, and those scarcely articulate, were uttered by the Prince, when a noise of people approaching from the palace startled us. The moon was now rising; and the idea of being overheard, or of his Royal Highness being seen out at so unusual an hour, terrified the whole group. After a few more words of the most affectionate nature uttered by the Prince, we parted, and Lord Malden and myself returned to the island. The Prince never quitted the avenue, nor the presence of the Duke of York, during the whole of this short meeting. Alas! My friend, if my mind was before influenced by esteem, it was now awakened to the most enthusiastic admiration. The rank of the Prince no longer chilled into awe that being who now considered him as the lover and the friend. The graces of his person, the irresistible sweetness of his smile, the tenderness of his melodious yet manly voice, will be remembered by me till every vision of this changing scene shall be forgotten.

"Many and frequent were the interviews which afterwards took place at this romantic spot; our walks sometimes continued till past midnight; the Duke of York and Lord Malden were always of the party; our conversation was composed of general topics. The Prince had from his infancy been wholly secluded, and naturally took much pleasure in conversing about the busy world, its manners and pursuits, characters and scenery. Nothing could be more delightful or more rational than our mid-night perambulations. I always wore a dark-coloured habit, the rest of our party generally wrapped themselves in great-coats to disguise them, excepting the Duke of York, who almost universally alarmed us by the display of a *buff* coat, the most conspicuous colour he could have selected for an adventure of this nature. The polished and fascinating ingenuousness of his Royal Highness's manners contributed not a little to enliven our promenades. He sung with exquisite taste, and the tones of his voice breaking on the silence of the night have often appeared to my entranced senses like more than mortal melody. Often have I lamented the distance which destiny had placed between us. How would my soul have idolised such a *husband* Alas! how often, in the ardent enthusiasm of my soul, have I formed the wish that that being were *mine alone* to whom partial millions were to look up for protection.

"The Duke of York was now on the eve of quitting the country for Hanover; the Prince was also on the point of receiving his first establishment; and the apprehension that his attachment to a married woman might injure his Royal Highness in the opinion of the world, rendered the caution which we invariably observed of the utmost importance. A considerable time elapsed in these delightful scenes of visionary happiness. The Prince's attachment seemed to increase daily, and I considered myself as the most blest of human beings. During some time we had enjoyed our meetings in the neighbourhood of Kew, and I now only looked forward to the adjusting of his Royal Highness's establishment for the public avowal of our mutual attachment.

"I had relinquished my profession. The last night of my appearance on the stage, I represented the character of Sir Harry Revel, in the comedy of The Miniature Picture, written by Lady Craven;[1] and The Irish Widow. On entering the green-room, I informed Mr. Moody, who played in the farce, that I should appear no more after that night; and, endeavouring to smile while I sung, I repeated–

> "'Oh joy to you all in full measure,
> So wishes and prays Widow Brady! '

which were the last lines of my song in The Irish Widow. This effort to conceal the emotion I felt on quitting a profession I enthusiastically loved, was of short duration, and I burst into tears on my appearance. My regret at recollecting that I was treading for the last time the boards where I had so often received the most gratifying testimonies of public approbation; where mental exertion had been emboldened by private worth; that I was flying from a happy certainty, perhaps to pursue the phantom disappointment, nearly overwhelmed my faculties, and for some time deprived me of the power of articulation. Fortunately, the person on the stage with me had to begin the scene, which allowed me time to collect myself. I went, however, mechanically dull through the business of the evening, and notwithstanding the cheering expressions and applause of the audience, I was several times near fainting.

"The daily prints now indulged the malice of my enemies by the most scandalous paragraphs respecting the Prince of Wales and myself. I found it was now too late to stop the hourly augmenting torrent of abuse that was poured upon me from all quarters. Whenever I appeared in public, I was overwhelmed by the gazing of the multitude. I was frequently obliged to quit Ranelagh, owing to the crowd which staring curiosity had assembled round my box; and, even in the streets of the metropolis I scarcely ventured to enter a shop without experiencing the greatest inconvenience. Many hours have I waited till the crowd dispersed which surrounded my carriage, in expectation of my quitting the shop. I cannot suppress a smile at the absurdity of such proceeding, when I remember that, during nearly three seasons, I was almost every night upon the stage, and that I had then been near five years with Mr. Robinson at every fashionable place of entertainment. You, my dear sir, in your quiet haunts of transatlantic simplicity, will find some difficulty in reconciling these things to your mind–these unaccountable instances of national absurdity. Yet, so it is. I am well assured, that were a being possessed of more than human endowments to visit this country, it would experience indifference, if not total neglect, while a less worthy mortal might be worshipped as the idol of its day, if whispered into notoriety by the comments of the multitude. But, thank Heaven! my heart was not formed in the mould of callous effrontery. I shuddered at the gulf before me, and felt small gratification in the knowledge of having taken a step, which many who condemned would have been no less willing to imitate had they been placed in the same situation.

"Previous to my first interview with his Royal Highness, in one of his letters I was astonished to find a bond of the most solemn and binding nature, containing a promise of the sum of twenty thousand pounds, to be paid at the period of his Royal Highness's coming of age.

"This paper was signed by the Prince, and sealed with the royal arms. It was expressed in terms so liberal, so voluntary, so marked by true affection, that I had scarcely power to read it. My tears, excited by the most agonising conflicts, obscured the letters, and nearly blotted out those sentiments which will be impressed upon my mind till the latest period of my existence. Still, I felt shocked and mortified at the indelicate idea of entering into any pecuniary engagements with a Prince, on whose establishment I relied for the enjoyment of all that would render life desirable. I was surprised at receiving it; the idea of interest had never entered my mind. Secure in the possession of his heart, I had in that delightful certainty counted all my future treasure. I had refused many splendid gifts which his Royal Highness had proposed ordering for me at Grey's and other jewellers. The Prince presented to me a few trifling ornaments, in the whole their value not exceeding one hundred guineas. Even these, on our separation, I returned to his Royal Highness through the hands of General Lake.

"The period now approached that was to destroy all the fairy visions which had filled my mind with dreams of happiness. At the moment when everything was preparing for his Royal Highness's establishment, when I looked impatiently for the arrival of that day in which I might behold my adored friend gracefully receiving the acclamations of his future subjects; when I might enjoy the public protection of that being for whom I gave up all, I received a letter from his Royal Highness, a cold and unkind letter–briefly informing me that 'We must meet no more.'

"And now, my friend, suffer me to call God to witness, that I was unconscious why this decision had taken place in his Royal Highness's mind. Only two days previous to this letter being written I had seen the Prince at Kew, and his affection appeared to be boundless as it was undiminished.

"Amazed, afflicted, beyond the power of utterance, I wrote immediately to his Royal Highness, requiring an explanation. He remained silent. Again I wrote, but received no elucidation of this most cruel and extraordinary mystery. The Prince was then at Windsor. I set out in a small pony phaeton, wretched, and unaccompanied by any one except my postillion (a child of nine years of age). It was near dark when we quitted Hyde Park Corner. On my arrival at Hounslow the innkeeper informed me that every carriage which had passed the heath for the last ten nights had been attacked and rifled. I confess the idea of personal danger had no terrors for my mind in the state it then was, and the possibility of annihilation, divested of the crime of suicide, encouraged rather than diminished my determination of proceeding. We had scarcely reached the middle of the heath when my horses were startled by the sudden appearance of a man rushing from the side of the road. The boy on perceiving him instantly spurred his pony, and, by a sudden bound of our light vehicle, the ruffian missed his grasp at the front rein. We now proceeded at full speed, while the footpad ran endeavouring to overtake us. At length, my horses fortunately outrunning the perseverance of the assailant, we reached the first 'Magpie,' a small inn on the heath, in safety. The alarm which, in spite of my resolution, this adventure had created, was augmented on my recollecting, for the first time, that I had then in my black stock a brilliant stud of very considerable value, which could only have been possessed by the robber by strangling the wearer.

"If my heart palpitated with joy at my escape from assassination, a circumstance soon after occurred that did not tend to quiet my emotion. This was the appearance of Mr. H. Meynell and Mrs. A––. My foreboding soul instantly beheld a rival, and, with jealous eagerness, interpreted the hitherto inexplicable conduct of the Prince from his having frequently expressed his wish to know that lady.

"On my arrival the Prince would not see me. My agonies were now undescribable. I consulted with Lord Malden and the Duke of Dorset, whose honourable mind and truly disinterested friendship had on many occasions been exemplified towards me. They were both at a loss to divine any cause of this sudden change in the Prince's feelings. The Prince of Wales had hitherto assiduously sought opportunities to distinguish me more publicly than was prudent in his Royal Highness's situation. This was in the month of August. On the 4th of the preceding June I went, by his desire, into the Chamberlain's box at the birth-night ball; the distressing observation of the circle was drawn towards the part of the box in which I sat by the marked and injudicious attentions of his Royal Highness. I had not been arrived many minutes before I witnessed a singular species of fashionable coquetry. Previous to his Highness's beginning his minuet, I perceived a woman of high rank select from the bouquet which she wore two rosebuds, which she gave to the Prince, as he afterwards informed me, 'emblematical of herself and him.' I observed his Royal Highness immediately beckon to a nobleman, who has since formed a part of his establishment, and, looking most earnestly at me, whisper a few words, at the same time presenting to him his newly-acquired trophy. In a few moments Lord C— entered the Chamberlain's box, and, giving the rosebuds into my hands, informed me that he was commissioned by the Prince to do so. I placed them in my bosom, and, I confess, felt proud of the power by which I thus publicly mortified an exalted rival. His Royal Highness now avowedly distinguished me at all public places of entertainment, at the King's hunt near Windsor, at the reviews, and at the theatres. The Prince only seemed happy in evincing his affection towards me.

"How terrible, then, was the change to my feelings! And I again most solemnly repeat that I was totally ignorant of any just cause for so sudden an alteration.

"My 'good-natured friends'now carefully informed me of the multitude of secret enemies who were ever employed in estranging the Prince's mind from me. So fascinating, so illustrious a lover could not fail to excite the envy of my own sex. Women of all descriptions were emulous of attracting his Royal Highness's attention. Alas! I had neither *rank* nor power to oppose such adversaries. Every engine of female malice was set in motion to destroy my repose, and every petty calumny was repeated with tenfold embellishments. Tales of the most infamous and glaring falsehood were invented, and I was again assailed by pamphlets, by paragraphs, and caricatures, and all the artillery of slander, while the only being to whom I then looked up for protection was so situated as to be unable to afford it.

"Thus perplexed, I wrote to you, my friend, and implored your advice. But you were far away; your delighted soul was absorbed in cherishing the plant of human liberty, which has since blossomed with independent splendour over your happy provinces. Eagerly did I wait for the arrival of the packet, but no answer was returned. In the anguish of my soul I once more addressed the Prince of Wales; I complained, perhaps too vehemently, of his injustice; of the calumnies which had been by my enemies fabricated against me, of the falsehood of which he was but too sensible. I conjured him to render me justice. He did so; he wrote me a most eloquent letter, disclaiming the causes alleged by a calumniating world, and fully acquitting me of the charges which had been propagated to destroy me.

"I resided now in Cork Street, Burlington Gardens. The house, which was neat, but by no means splendid, had recently been fitted up for the reception of the Countess of Derby, on her separation from her lord. My situation now every hour became more irksome. The Prince still unkindly persisted in withdrawing himself from my society. I was now deeply involved in debt, which I despaired of ever having the power to discharge. I had quitted both my husband and my profession. The retrospect was dreadful!

"My estrangement from the Prince was now the theme of public animadversion, while the newly invigorated shafts of my old enemies, the daily prints, were again hurled upon my defenceless head with tenfold fury. The regrets of Mr. Robinson, now that he had *lost* me, became insupportable; he constantly wrote to me in the language of unbounded affection, nor did he fail, when he met, to express his agony at our separation, and even a wish for our reunion.

"I had, at one period, resolved on returning to my profession; but some friends whom I consulted dreaded that the public would not suffer my reappearance on the stage. This idea intimidated me, and precluded my efforts for that independence of which my romantic credulity had robbed me. I was thus fatally induced to relinquish what would have proved an ample and honourable resource for myself and my child. My debts accumulated to near seven thousand pounds. My creditors, whose insulting illiberality could only be squalled by their unbounded impositions, hourly assailed me.

"I was, in the meantime, wholly neglected by the Prince, while the assiduities of Lord Malden daily increased. I had no other friend on whom I could rely for assistance or protection. When I say protection, I would not be understood to mean *pecuniary* assistance, Lord Malden being, at the time alluded to, even poorer than myself–the death of his lordship's grandmother, Lady Frances Coningsby, had not then placed him above the penury of his own small income.

"Lord Malden's attentions to me again exposed him to all the humiliation of former periods. The Prince assured me once more of his wishes to renew our former friendship and affection, and urged me to meet him at the house of Lord Malden in Clarges Street. I was at this period little less than frantic, deeply involved in debt, persecuted by my enemies, and perpetually reproached by my relations. I would joyfully have resigned an existence now become to me an intolerable burthen; yet my pride was not less than my sorrow, and I resolved, whatever my heart might suffer, to wear a placid countenance when I met the inquiring glances of my triumphant enemies.

"After much hesitation, by the advice of Lord Malden, I consented to meet his Royal Highness. He accosted me with every appearance of tender attachment, declaring that he had never for one moment ceased to love me, but that I had many concealed enemies, who were exerting every effort to undermine me. We passed some hours in the most friendly and delightful conversation, and I began to flatter myself that all our differences were adjusted. But what words can express my surprise and chagrin, when, on meeting his Royal Highness the *very next day* in Hyde Park, he turned his head to avoid seeing me, and even affected *not to know me!*

"Overwhelmed by this blow, my distress knew no limits. Yet *heaven* can witness the truth of my assertion, even in this moment of complete despair, when oppression bowed me to the earth, I blamed not the Prince. I did then, and ever shall, consider his mind as nobly and honourably organised, nor could I teach myself to believe that a heart, the seat of so many virtues, could possibly become inhuman and unjust. I had been taught from my infancy to believe that elevated stations are surrounded by delusive visions, which glitter but to dazzle, like an unsubstantial meteor, and flatter to betray. With legions of these phantoms it has been my fate to encounter; I have been unceasingly marked by their persecutions, and shall at length become their victim."

Here the narrative of Mrs. Robinson breaks off, with some reflections to which the recital had given rise. Though diligent search has been made to elucidate the obscurity in which the preceding events are involved, but little information has been gained. All that can be learned with certainty is her final separation from the Prince of Wales in the year 1781.

The genius and engaging manners of Mrs. Robinson, who was still very young, had procured her the friendship of many of the most enlightened men of this age and country; her house was the rendezvous of talents. While yet unconscious of the powers of her mind, which had scarcely then unfolded itself, she was honoured with the acquaintance and esteem of Sir Joshua Reynolds, Messrs. Sheridan, Burke, Henderson, Wilkes, Sir John Elliot, &c., men of distinguished talents and character. But though surrounded by the wise, the witty, and the gay, her mind, naturally pensive, was still devoured by secret sorrow; neither could the blandishments of flattery, nor the soothings of friendship, extract the arrow that rankled in her heart. Involved beyond the power of extrication, she determined on quitting England, and making a tour to Paris.

To desert her country, to fly like a wretched fugitive, or to become a victim to the malice, and swell the triumph of her enemies, were the only alternatives that seemed to present themselves. Flight was humiliating and dreadful, but to remain in England was impracticable. The terrors and struggles of her mind became almost intolerable, and nearly deprived her of reason. The establishment of the Prince had now taken place; to him, for whom she had made every sacrifice, and to whom she owed her present embarrassments, she conceived herself entitled to appeal for redress. She wrote to his Royal Highness, but her letter remained unanswered. The business was at length submitted to the arbitration of Mr. Fox, and, in 1783, her claims were adjusted by the grant of an annuity of five hundred pounds, the moiety of which was to descend to her daughter at her decease. This settlement was to be considered as an equivalent for the bond of twenty thousand pounds given by the Prince to Mrs. Robinson, to be paid on his establishment, as a consideration for the *resignation of a lucrative profession at the particular request of his Royal Highness* To many persons the assurance of an independence would have operated as a consolation for the sufferings and difficulties by which it had been procured; but the spirit of Mrs. Robinson bent not to a situation which the delicacy of her feelings led her to consider as a splendid degradation.

About this period Mrs. Robinson, notwithstanding the change in her affairs, determined to visit Paris, to amuse her mind and beguile her thoughts from the recollection of past scenes. Having procured letters of introduction to some agreeable French families, and also to Sir John Lambert, resident English banker at Paris, she quitted London, with the resolution of passing two months in the gay and brilliant metropolis of France. Sir John Lambert, on being informed of her arrival, exerted himself to procure for her commodious apartments, a *remise,* a box at the opera, with all the fashionable and expensive *et-ceteras* with which an inexperienced English traveller is immediately provided.

This venerable *chevalier* united to the cordiality of the English character the *bienfaisance* of a Frenchman–every hour was devoted to the amusement of his admired guest, who came to him highly recommended. Parties were, with the most flattering assiduity, formed for the different *spectacles* and places of public entertainment. A brilliant assemblage of illustrious visitors failed not to grace at the opera the box of *la belle Anglaise.*

A short time after the arrival of Mrs. Robinson at Paris, the Duke of Orleans and his gallant friend and associate, the Duke de Lauzun (afterwards Duke de Biron) were presented to her by Sir John Lambert. This unfortunate prince, with all the volatility of the national character, disgraced human nature by his vices, while the elegance of his manners rendered him a model to his contemporaries.

The Duke of Orleans immediately professed himself devoted to the fair stranger. His libertine manners, the presumption with which he declared his determination to triumph over the heart of Mrs. Robinson, assisted to defend her against him; and, while he failed to dazzle her imagination by his magnificence, he disgusted her by his *hauteur.*

The most enchanting *fêtes* were given at Mousseau, a villa belonging to the Duke of Orleans near Paris, at which Mrs. Robinson invariably declined to appear. Brilliant races *à l'Anglaise* were exhibited on the plains *des Sablons,* to captivate the attention of the inexorable *Anglaise.* On the birthday of Mrs. Robinson a new effort was made to subdue her aversion and to obtain her regard. A rural *fête* was appointed in the gardens of Mousseau, when this beautiful *Pandæmonium* of splendid profligacy was, at an unusual expense, decorated with boundless luxury.

In the evening, amidst a magnificent illumination, every tree displayed the initials of *la belle Anglaise,* composed of coloured lamps, interwoven with wreaths of artificial flowers. Politeness compelled Mrs. Robinson to grace with her presence a *fête* instituted to her honour. She, however, took the precaution of selecting for her companion a German lady, then resident at Paris, while the venerable chevalier Lambert attended them as a *chaperon*.

M.ʳ Robinson.
from an Engraving by Condell after Dance.

Some days after the celebration of this festival, the Queen of France signified her intention of dining in public, for the first time after her *accouchement* with the Duke of Normandy, afterwards Dauphin. The duke brought to Mrs. Robinson a message from the Queen, expressing a wish that *la belle Anglaise* might be induced to appear at the *grand couvert*. Mrs. Robinson, not less solicitous to behold the lovely Marie Antoinette, gladly availed herself of the intimation, and immediately began to prepare for the important occasion. The most tasteful ornaments of Mademoiselle Bertin, the reigning milliner, were procured to adorn a form that, rich in native beauty, needed little embellishment. A pale green lustring train and body, with a tiffany petticoat, festooned with bunches of the most delicate lilac, were chosen by Mrs. Robinson for her appearance, while a plume of white feathers adorned her head;

the native roses of her cheeks, glowing with health and youth, were stained, in conformity to the fashion of the French Court, with the deepest *rouge*.

On the arrival of the fair foreigner, the Duke d'Orleans quitted the *King* on whom he was then in waiting, to procure her a place, where the Queen might have an opportunity of observing those charms by the fame of which her curiosity had been awakened.

The *grand convert*, at which the King acquitted himself with more alacrity than grace, afforded a magnificent display of epicurean luxury. The Queen ate nothing. The slender crimson cord, which drew a line of separation between the royal epicures and the gazing plebeians, was at the distance but of a few feet from the table. A small space divided the Queen from Mrs. Robinson, whom the constant observation and loudly whispered encomiums of Her Majesty most oppressively flattered. She appeared to survey, with peculiar attention, a miniature of the Prince of Wales, which Mrs. Robinson wore on her bosom, and of which, on the ensuing day, she commissioned the Duke of Orleans to request the loan. Perceiving Mrs. Robinson gaze with admiration on her white and polished arms, as she drew on her gloves, the Queen again uncovered them, and leaned for a few moments on her hand. The Duke, on returning the picture, gave to the fair owner a purse, netted by the hand of Antoinette, and which she had commissioned him to present, from her, to *la belle Anglaise*. Mrs. Robinson not long after these events quitted Paris, and returned to her native country.

In 1784 her fate assumed a darker hue. She was attacked by a malady, to which she had nearly fallen a victim. By an imprudent exposure to the night air in travelling, when, exhausted by fatigue and mental anxiety, she slept in a chaise with the windows open, she brought on a fever, which confined her to her bed during six months. The disorder terminated at the conclusion of that period *in a violent rheumatism, which progressively deprived her of the use of her limbs.* Thus, at four-and-twenty years of age, in the pride of youth and the bloom of beauty, was this lovely and unfortunate woman reduced to a state of more than infantile helplessness. Yet, even under so severe a calamity, the powers of her mind and the elasticity of her spirits triumphed over the weakness of her frame. This check to the pleasures and vivacity of youth, by depriving her of external resource, led her to the more assiduous cultivation and development of her talents. But the resignation with which she had submitted to one of the severest of human calamities gave place to hope, on the assurance of her physician, that by the mild air of a more southern climate she might probably be restored to health and activity.

The favourite wish of her heart, that of beholding her relations, from whom she had been so many years divided, it was now in her power to gratify. From her elder brother she had frequently received invitations, the most pressing and affectionate, to quit for ever a country where an unprotected woman rarely fails to become the victim of calumny and persecution, and to take shelter in the bosom of domestic tranquillity, where peace, to which she had long been a stranger, might still await her. Delighted with the idea of combining with the object of her travels an acquisition so desirable, and after which her exhausted heart panted, she eagerly embraced the proposal, and set out to Paris, with the resolution of proceeding to Leghorn. But a letter, on her arrival, from her physician, prescribing the warm baths of Aix-la-Chapelle in Germany, as a certain restorative for her complaints, frustrated her plans Once more she proceeded in melancholy pursuit of that blessing which she was destined never more to obtain.

During her sojourn at Aix-la-Chapelle, a dawn of comparative tranquillity soothed her spirits. Secure from the machinations of her enemies, she determined, though happiness seemed no more within her reach, to endeavour to be content. The assiduities and attentions shown her by all ranks of people presented a striking medium between the volatility and libertine homage offered to her at Paris, and the persevering malignity which had followed her in her native land. Her beauty, the affecting state of her health, the attraction of her manners, and the powers of her mind, interested every heart in her favour; while the meekness with which she submitted to her fate excited an admiration not less fervent, and more genuine, than her charms in the full blaze of their power had ever extorted.

Among the many illustrious and enlightened persons then resident at Aix-la-Chapelle who honoured Mrs. Robinson by their friendship, she received from the late amiable and unfortunate Duke and Duchess du Châtelet peculiar marks of distinction. The Duke had, while ambassador in England, been the friend and associate of the learned Lord Mansfield; his Duchess, the *élève* of Voltaire, claimed as her godmother Gabrielle Emilia, Baroness du Châtelet, so celebrated by that lively and admirable writer. This inestimable family, consisting of the Duke and Duchess, their nephews the Counts de Damas, and a niece married to the Duke de Simianne, were indefatigable in their efforts to solace the affliction and amuse the mind of their fair friend. Balls, concerts, rural breakfasts, succeeded to each other in gay and attractive variety; the happy effects produced on the health and spirits of Mrs. Robinson were considered by this English family as an ample compensation for their solicitude. When compelled by severer paroxysms of her malady to seclude herself from their society, a thousand kind stratagems were planned and executed to relieve her sufferings, or soften the dejection to which they unavoidably gave rise. Sometimes, on entering her dark and melancholy bath, the gloom of which was increased by high grated windows, she beheld the surface of the water covered with rose-leaves, while the vapour baths were impregnated with aromatic odours. The younger part of the family, when pain deprived Mrs. Robinson of rest, frequently passed the night beneath her windows, charming her sufferings and beguiling her of her sorrows, by singing her favourite airs to the accompaniment of the mandolin.

Thus, in despite of sickness, glided away two agreeable winters, when the transient gleam of brightness became suddenly obscured, and her prospects involved in deeper shade.

About this period Mrs. Robinson had the misfortune to lose her brave and respected father—a blow as forcible as unexpected, which nearly shook her faculties, and, for a time, wholly overwhelmed her spirits. Captain Darby had, on the failure of his fortunes, been presented to the command of a small ordnance vessel, through the interest of some of his noble associates in the Indian expedition. Not having been regularly bred to the sea, this was the only naval appointment which he could receive. Enthusiastically attached to his profession, he omitted no occasion of signalising himself. The siege of Gibraltar, in the year 1783, afforded to him an opportunity after which he had long panted, when his small vessel and gallant crew extorted by their courage and exertions the admiration and applause of the fleet. Having fought till his rigging was nearly destroyed, he turned his attention to the sinking Spaniards, whom he sought to snatch from the flaming wrecks, floating around him in all directions, and had the satisfaction to preserve, though at the hazard of his life, some hundreds of his fellow beings. The vessel of Captain Darby was the first that reached the rock by nearly an hour. On his landing, General Elliot received and embraced him with the plaudits due to his gallant conduct.

In the presence of his officers, the general lamented that so brave a man had not been bred to a profession to which his intrepidity would have done distinguished honour. To this eulogium he added, that, with the courage of a lion, Captain Darby possessed the firmness of the rock which he had so bravely defended.

To his care was entrusted by the commander a *copy* of the despatches, which Captain Darby delivered four-and-twenty hours *before the arrival* of the regular vessel. For this diligence, and the conduct which had preceded it, he received the *thanks* of the Board of Admiralty, while on the other captain was bestowed the more substantial recompense of five hundred pounds. An injustice so glaring was not calculated to lessen Captain Darby's distaste for England, which he quitted, after taking of his unhappy family an affectionate farewell.

At sixty-two years of age, he set out to regain in a foreign country the fortune he had sacrificed in the service of his own. With powerful recommendations from the Duke of Dorset and the Count de Simolin, he proceeded to Petersburg. From the Count de Simolin he continued to experience, till the latest period of his existence, a steady and zealous friendship. Captain Darby had been but two years in the Russian imperial service, when he was promoted to the command of a seventy-four gun ship, with a promise of the appointment of admiral on the first vacancy. On the 5th of December, 1785, death put a stop to his career. He was buried with military honours, and attended to the grave by his friends, Admiral Greig, the Counts Czernichef and De Simolin, with the officers of the fleet. [1]

This honourable testimony to her father's worth was the only consolation remaining to his daughter, whose enfeebled health and broken spirits sunk beneath these repeated strokes.

During the four succeeding years of the life of Mrs. Robinson, but few events occurred worthy of remark. In search of lost health, which she had so long and vainly pursued, she determined to repair to the baths of St. Amand, in Flanders, those receptacles of loathsome mud, and of reptiles, unknown to other soils, which fasten on the bodies of those who bathe. Mrs. Robinson made many visits to these distasteful ditches before she could prevail on herself to enter them. Neither the example of her fellow-sufferers, nor the assurance of cures performed by their wonderful efficacy, could for a long time overcome her disgust. At length, solicitude for the restoration of her health, added to the earnest remonstrances of her friends, determined her on making the effort. For the purpose of being near the baths, which must be entered an hour before the rising of the sun, she hired a small but beautiful cottage near the spring, where she passed the summer of 1787. These peaceful vales and venerable woods were, at no distant period, destined to become the seat of war and devastation, and the very cottage in which Mrs. Robinson resided was converted into the headquarters of a Republican French general.

Every endeavour to subdue her disorder proving ineffectual, Mrs. Robinson relinquished her melancholy and fruitless pursuit, and resolved once more to return to her native land. Proceeding through Paris, she reached England in the beginning of 1787, from which period may be dated the commencement of her literary career. On her arrival in London she was affectionately received by the few friends whose attachment neither detraction nor adverse fortunes could weaken or estrange. During an absence of five years death had made inroads in the little circle of her connections; many of those whose idea had been her solace in affliction, and whose welcome she had delighted to anticipate, were now, alas! no more. [1]

Once more established in London, and surrounded by social and rational friends, Mrs. Robinson began to experience comparative tranquillity. The Prince of Wales, with his brother the Duke of York, frequently honoured her residence with their presence; but the state of her health, which required more repose, added to the indisposition of her daughter, who was threatened by a consumptive disorder, obliged her to withdraw to a situation of greater retirement. Maternal solicitude for a beloved and only child now wholly engaged her attention; her assiduities were incessant and exemplary for the restoration of a being to whom she had given life, and to whom she was fondly devoted.

In the course of the summer she was ordered by her physician to Brighthelmstone, for the benefit of sea bathing. During hours of tedious watching over the health of her suffering child, Mrs. Robinson beguiled her anxiety by contemplating the ocean, whose successive waves, breaking upon the shore, beat against the wall of their little garden. To a mind naturally susceptible, and tinctured by circumstances with sadness, this occupation afforded a melancholy pleasure, which could scarcely be relinquished without regret. Whole nights were passed by Mrs. Robinson at her window in deep meditation, contrasting with her present situation the scenes of her former life.

Mrs Robinson
from an Engraving by ... after Reynolds

Every device which a kind and skilful nurse could invent to cheer and amuse her charge was practised by this affectionate mother, during the melancholy period of her daughter's confinement. In the intervals of more active exertion, the silence of a sick chamber proving favourable to the muse, Mrs. Robinson poured forth those poetic effusions which have done so much honour to her genius and decked her tomb with unfading laurels. Conversing one evening with Mr. Richard Burke,[1] respecting the facility with which modern poetry was composed, Mrs. Robinson repeated nearly the whole of those beautiful lines, which were afterwards given to the public, addressed—*"To him who will understand them."*

LINES TO HIM WHO WILL UNDERSTAND THEM.

THOU art no more my bosom's friend;
Here must the sweet delusion end,
That charm'd my senses many a year,

Through smiling summers, winters drear.
O, friendship! am I doom'd to find
Thou art a phantom of the mind?
A glitt'ring shade, an empty name,
An air-born vision's vap'rish flame?
And yet, the dear deceit so long
Has wak'd to joy my matin song,
Has bid my tears forget to flow,
Chas'd ev'ry pain, soothed ev'ry woe;
That truth, unwelcome to my ear,
Swells the deep sigh, recalls the tear,
Gives to the sense the keenest smart,
Checks the warm pulses of the heart,
Darkens my fate, and steals away
Each gleam of joy through life's sad day.

 Britain, farewell! I quit thy shore,
My native country charms no more;
No guide to mark the toilsome road;
No destin'd clime; no fix'd abode:
Alone and sad, ordain'd to trace
The vast expanse of endless space;
To view, upon the mountain's height,
Through varied shades of glimm'ring light,
The distant landscape fade away
In the last gleam of parting day:
Or, on the quiv'ring lucid stream,
To watch the pale moon's silv'ry beam;
Or when, in sad and plaintive strains
The mournful Philomel complains,
In dulcet notes bewails her fate,
And murmurs for her absent mate;
Inspir'd by sympathy divine,
I'll weep her woes–for they are mine.
Driven by my fate, where'er I go
O'er burning plains, o'er hills of snow,
Or on the bosom of the wave,

The howling tempest doom'd to brave,–
Where'er my lonely course I bend,
Thy image shall my steps attend;
Each object I am doom'd to see,
Shall bid remem'brance picture thee.
Yes; I shall view thee in each flow'r,
That changes with the transient hour:
Thy wand'ring fancy I shall find
Borne on the wings of every wind:
Thy wild impetuous passions trace
O'er the white wave's tempestuous space:
In every changing season prove
An emblem of thy wav'ring love.

  Torn from my country, friends, and you,
The world lies open to my view;
New objects shall my mind engage;
I will explore th' historic page;
Sweet poetry shall soothe my soul;
Philosophy each pang control:
The muse I'll seek– her lambent fire
My soul's quick senses shall inspire;
With finer nerves my heart shall beat,
Touch'd by heaven's own promethean heat;
Italia's gales shall bear my song
In soft-link'd notes her woods among;
Upon the blue hill's misty side,
Thro' trackless deserts waste and wide,
O'er craggy rocks, whose torrents flow
Upon the silver sands below.
Sweet land of melody! 'tis thine
The softest passions to refine;
Thy myrtle groves, thy melting strains,
Shall harmonize and soothe my pains,

Nor will I cast one thought behind,
On foes relentless, friends unkind:
I feel, I feel their poison'd dart

Pierce the life-nerve within my heart;
'Tis mingled with the vital heat
That bids my throbbing pulses beat;
Soon shall that vital heat be o'er,
Those throbbing pulses beat no more!
No–I will breathe the spicy gale;
Plunge the clear stream, new health exhale;
O'er my pale cheek diffuse the rose,
And drink oblivion to my woes.

This *improvisatore* produced in her auditor not less surprise than admiration, when solemnly assured by its author that this was the first time of its being repeated. Mr. Burke [1] entreated her to commit the poem to writing, a request which was readily complied with. Mrs. Robinson had afterwards the gratification of finding this offspring of her genius inserted in the Annual Register, with a flattering encomium from the pen of the eloquent and ingenious editor .

Mrs. Robinson continued to indulge in this solace for her dejected spirits, and in sonnets, elegies, and odes, displayed the powers and versatility of her mind. On one of these nights of melancholy inspiration she discovered from her window a small boat, struggling in the spray, which dashed against the wall of her garden. Presently two fishermen brought on shore in their arms a burthen, which, notwithstanding the distance, Mrs. Robinson perceived to be a human body, which the fishermen, after covering with a sail from their boat, left on the land and disappeared. But a short time elapsed before the men returned, bringing with them fuel, with which they vainly endeavoured to reanimate their unfortunate charge. Struck with a circumstance so affecting, which the stillness of the night rendered yet more impressive, Mrs. Robinson remained some time at her window motionless with horror. At length, recovering her recollection, she alarmed the family; but before they could gain the beach the men had again departed. The morning dawned, and day broke in upon the tragical scene. The bathers passed and repassed with little concern, while the corpse continued extended on the shore, not twenty yards from the Steine. During the course of the day many persons came to look on the body, which still remained unclaimed and unknown. Another day wore away and the corpse was unburied, the lord of the manor having refused to a fellow-being a grave in which his bones might decently repose, alleging as an excuse, *that he did not belong to that parish. Mrs. Robinson*, humanely indignant at the scene which passed, exerted herself, but without success, to procure by subscription a small sum for performing the last duties to a wretched outcast. Unwilling, by an ostentatious display of her name, to offend the higher and more fastidious female powers, she presented to the fishermen her own contribution, and declined farther to interfere. The affair dropped; and the body of the stranger, being dragged to the cliff, was covered by a heap of stones, without the tribute of a sigh or the ceremony of a prayer.

These circumstances made on the mind of Mrs. Robinson a deep and lasting impression; even at a distant period she could not repeat them without horror and indignation. This incident gave rise to the poem entitled "The Haunted Beach," written but a few months before her death.

In the winter of 1790, Mrs. Robinson entered into a poetical correspondence with Mr. Robert Merry, under the fictitious names of "Laura," and "Laura Maria"; Mr. Merry assuming the title of "Della Crusca." [1]

Mrs. Robinson now proceeded in her literary career with redoubled ardour; but, dazzled by the false metaphors and rhapsodical extravagance of some contemporary writers, she suffered her judgment to be misled and her taste to be perverted: an error of which she became afterwards sensible. During her poetical disguise, many complimentary poems were addressed to her; several ladies of the Blue Stocking Club, while Mrs. Robinson remained unknown, even ventured to admire, nay more, to recite her productions in their learned and critical *coterie.*

The attention which this novel species of correspondence excited, and the encomiums which were passed on her poems, could not fail to gratify the pride of the writer, who sent her next performance, with her own signature, to the paper published under the title of *The World* avowing herself at the same time the author of the lines signed "Laura," and "Laura Maria." This information being received by Mr. Bell, though a professed admirer of the genius of Mrs. Robinson, with some degree of scepticism, he replied, "That the poem with which Mrs. Robinson had honoured him was *vastly pretty;* but that he was well acquainted with the author of the productions alluded to." Mrs. Robinson, a little disgusted at this incredulity, immediately sent for Mr. Bell, whom she found means to convince of her veracity, and of his own injustice.

In 1791 Mrs. Robinson produced her quarto poem, entitled "Ainsi va le Monde." This work, containing three hundred and fifty lines, was written in twelve hours, as a reply to Mr. Merry's "Laurel of Liberty," which was sent to Mrs. Robinson on a Saturday; on the *Tuesday following* answer was *composed and given to the public.*

Encouraged by popular approbation beyond her most sanguine hopes, Mrs. Robinson now published her first essay in prose, in the romance of Vancenza, of which the whole edition was *sold in one day,* and of which five impressions have since followed. It must be confessed that this production owed its popularity to the celebrity of the author's name, and the favourable impression of her talents given to the public by her poetical compositions, rather than to its intrinsic merit. In the same year the poems of Mrs. Robinson were collected and published in one volume. The names of nearly six hundred subscribers, of the most distinguished rank and talents, graced the list which precedes the work.

The mind of Mrs. Robinson, beguiled by these pursuits from preying upon itself, became gradually reconciled to the calamitous state of her health; the mournful certainty of total and incurable lameness, while yet in the bloom and summer of life, was alleviated by the consciousness of intellectual resource, and by the activity of a fertile fancy. In 1791 she passed the greater part of the summer at Bath, occupied in lighter poetical compositions. But even from this relief she was now for a while debarred: the perpetual exercise of the imagination and intellect, added to a uniform and sedentary life, affected the system of her nerves, and contributed to debilitate her frame. She was prohibited by her physician, not merely from committing her thoughts to paper, but, had it been possible, from thinking at all. No truant, escaped from school, could receive more pleasure in eluding a severe master, than did Mrs. Robinson, when, the vigilance of her physician relaxing, she could once more resume her books and her pen.

As an example of the facility and rapidity with which she composed, the following anecdote may be given. Returning one evening from the bath, she beheld, a few paces before her chair, an elderly man, hurried along by a crowd of people, by whom he was pelted with mud and stones. His meek and unresisting deportment exciting her attention, she inquired what were his offences, and learned with pity and surprise that he was an unfortunate maniac, known only by the appellation of "mad Jemmy." The situation of this miserable being seized her imagination and became the subject of her attention. She would wait whole hours for the appearance of the poor maniac, and, whatever were her occupations, the voice of "mad Jemmy." was sure to allure her to the window. She would gaze upon his venerable but emaciated countenance with sensations of awe almost reverential, while the barbarous persecutions of the thoughtless crowd never failed to agonise her feelings.

One night after bathing, having suffered from her disorder more than usual pain, she swallowed, by order of her physician, near eighty drops of laudanum. Having slept for some hours, she awoke, and calling her daughter, desired her to take a pen and write what she should dictate. Miss Robinson, supposing that a request so unusual might proceed from the delirium excited by the opium, endeavoured in vain to dissuade her mother from her purpose. The spirit of inspiration was not to be subdued, and she repeated, throughout, the admirable poem of "The Maniac," [1] much faster than it could be committed to paper.

She lay, while dictating, with her eyes closed, apparently in the stupor which opium frequently produces, repeating like a person talking in her sleep. This affecting performance, produced in circumstances so singular, does no less credit to the genius than to the heart of the author.

On the ensuing morning Mrs. Robinson had only a confused idea of what had passed, nor could be convinced of the fact till the manuscript was produced. She declared that she had been dreaming of mad Jemmy throughout the night, but was perfectly unconscious of having been awake while she composed the poem, or of the circumstances narrated by her daughter.

Mrs. Robinson, in the following summer, determined on another continental tour, purposing to remain some time at Spa. She longed once more to experience the friendly greeting and liberal kindness which even her acknowledged talents had in her native country failed to procure. She quitted London in July, 1792, accompanied by her mother and daughter. The susceptible and energetic mind, fortunately for its possessor, is endowed with an elastic power, that enables it to rise again from the benumbing effects of those adverse strokes of fortune to which it is but too vulnerable. If a lively imagination add poignancy to disappointment, it also has in itself resources unknown to more equal temperaments. In the midst of the depressing feelings which Mrs. Robinson experienced in once more becoming a wanderer from her home, she courted the inspiration of the muse, and soothed, by the following beautiful stanzas, the melancholy sensations that oppressed her heart.

STANZAS

WRITTEN BETWEEN DOVER AND CALAIS,

JULY 20, 1792.

BOUNDING billow, cease thy motion,
Bear me not so swiftly o'er;
Cease thy roaring, foamy ocean,
I will tempt thy rage no more

Ah! within my bosom beating,
Varying passions wildly reign;
Love, with proud Resentment meeting,
Throbs by turns, of joy and pain.

Joy, that far from foes I wander,
Where their taunts can reach no more;
Pain, that woman's heart grows fonder
When her dream of bliss is o'er!

Love, by fickle fancy banish'd,
Spurn'd by hope, indignant flies;
Yet when love and hope are vanish'd,
Restless mem'ry never dies.

Far I go, where fate shall lead me,
Far across the troubled deep;
Where no stranger's ear shall heed me,
Where no eye for me shall weep.

Proud has been my fatal passion!
Proud my injured heart shall be!
While each thought, each inclination,
Still shall prove me worthy *thee!*

Not one sigh shall tell my story;
Not one tear my cheek shall stain;

Silent grief shall be my glory,–
Grief, that stoops not to complain!

Let the bosom prone to ranging,
Still by ranging seek a cure;
Mine disdains the thought of changing,
Proudly destin'd to endure.

Yet, ere far from all I treasur'd,
– ere I bid adieu;
Ere my days of pain are measur'd,
Take the song that's still thy due!

Yet, believe, no servile passions
Seek to charm thy vagrant mind;
Well I know thy inclinations,
Wav'ring as the passing wind.

I have lov'd thee,–dearly lov'd thee,
Through an age of worldly woe;
How ungrateful I have prov'd thee
Let my mournful exile show!

Ten long years of anxious sorrow,
Hour by hour I counted o'er;
Looking forward, till to-morrow,
Every day I lov'd thee more!

Pow'r and splendour could not charm me;
I no joy in wealth could see!
Nor could threats or fears alarm me,
Save the fear of losing thee!

When the storms of fortune press'd thee,
I have wept to see thee weep!
When relentless cares distress'd thee,
I have lull'd those cares to sleep!

When with thee, what ills could harm me?
Thou couldst every pang assuage;
But when absent, nought could charm me;
Every moment seem'd an age.

Fare thee well, ungrateful rover!
Welcome Gallia's hostile shore:
Now the breezes waft me over;
Now we part–TO MEET NO MORE.

On landing at Calais Mrs. Robinson hesitated whether to proceed. To travel through Flanders, then the seat of war, threatened too many perils to be attempted with impunity; she determined therefore for some time to remain at Calais, the insipid and spiritless amusements of which presented little either to divert her attention or engage her mind. Her time passed in listening to the complaints of the impoverished aristocrats, or in attending to the air-built projects of their triumphant adversaries. The arrival of travellers from England, or the return of those from Paris, alone diversified the scene, and afforded a resource to the curious and active inquirer.

The sudden arrival of her husband gave a turn to the feelings of Mrs. Robinson: he had crossed the Channel for the purpose of carrying back to England his daughter, whom he wished to present to a brother newly returned from the East Indies. Maternal conflicts shook on this occasion the mind of Mrs. Robinson, which hesitated between a concern for the interests of her beloved child, from whom she had never been separated, and the pain of parting from her. She resolved at length on accompanying her to England, and, with this view, quitted Calais on the memorable 2nd of September, 1792, [1] a day which will reflect on the annals of the Republic an indelible stain.

They had sailed but a few hours when the *arrêt* arrived, by which every British subject throughout France was restrained.

Mrs. Robinson rejoiced in her escape, and anticipated with delight the idea of seeing her daughter placed in wealthy protection, the great passport in her own country to honour and esteem. Miss Robinson received from her new relation the promise of protection and favour, upon condition that she renounced for ever the filial tie which united her to *both* parents. This proposal was rejected by the young lady with proper principle and becoming spirit.

In the year 1793 a little farce, entitled Nobody, was written by Mrs. Robinson. This piece, designed as a satire on female gamesters, was received at the theatre, the characters distributed, and preparations made for its exhibition. At this period one of the principal performers gave up her part, alleging that the piece was intended as a ridicule on her particular friend. Another actress also, though in "herself a host," was intimidated by a letter, informing her that "*Nobody* should be damned!" The author received likewise, on the same day, a scurrilous, indecent, and ill-disguised scrawl, signifying to her that the farce was already condemned. On the drawing up of the curtain, several persons in the galleries, whose liveries betrayed their employers, were heard to declare that they were sent to *do up* Nobody. Even women of distinguished rank hissed through their fans. Notwithstanding these maneuvers and exertions, the more rational part of the audience seemed inclined to hear before they passed judgment, and, with a firmness that never fails to awe, demanded that the piece should proceed. The first act was accordingly suffered without interruption; a song in the second being unfortunately encored, the malcontents once more ventured to raise their voices, and the malignity that had been forcibly suppressed burst forth with redoubled violence. For three nights the theatre presented a scene of confusion, when the authoress, after experiencing the gratification of a zealous and sturdy defence, thought proper wholly to withdraw the cause of contention. [1]

Mrs. Robinson in the course of this year lost her only remaining parent, whom she tenderly loved and sincerely lamented. Mrs. Darby expired in the house of her daughter, who, though by far

125

the least wealthy of her children, had proved herself through life the most attentive and affectionate. From the first hour of Mr. Darby's failure and estrangement from his family, Mrs. Robinson had been the protector and the support of her mother. Even when pressed herself by pecuniary embarrassment, it had been her pride and pleasure to shelter her widowed parent, and preserve her from inconvenience.

Mrs. Darby had two sons, merchants, wealthy and respected in the commercial world; but to these gentlemen Mrs. Robinson would never suffer her mother to apply for any assistance that was not voluntarily offered. The filial sorrow of Mrs. Robinson on her loss for many months affected her health; even to the latest hour of her life her grief appeared renewed when any object presented itself connected with the memory of her departed mother.

Few events of importance occurred during the five following years, excepting that through this period the friends of Mrs. Robinson observed with concern the gradual ravages which indisposition and mental anxiety were daily making upon her frame. An ingenuous, affectionate, susceptible heart is seldom favourable to the happiness of the possessor. It was the fate of Mrs. Robinson to be deceived where she most confided, to experience treachery and ingratitude where she had a title to kindness and a claim to support. Frank and unsuspicious, she suffered her conduct to be guided by the impulse of her feelings; and, by a too credulous reliance on the apparent attachment of those whom she loved, and in whom she delighted to trust, she laid herself open to the impositions of the selfish, and the stratagems of the crafty.

In 1799 her increasing involvements and declining health pressed heavily upon her mind. She had voluntarily relinquished those comforts and elegancies to which she had been accustomed; she had retrenched even her necessary expenses, and nearly secluded herself from society. Her physician had declared that by exercise only could her existence be prolonged; yet the narrowness of her circumstances obliged her to forego the only means by which it could be obtained. Thus, a prisoner in her own house, she was deprived of every solace but that which could be obtained by the activity of her mind, which at length sank under excessive exertion and inquietude.

Indisposition had for nearly five weeks confined her to her bed, when, after a night of extreme suffering and peril, through which her physician hourly expected her dissolution, she had sunk into a gentle and balmy sleep. At this instant her chamber door was forcibly pushed open, with a noise that shook her enfeebled frame nearly to annihilation, by two strange and ruffian-looking men, who entered with barbarous abruptness. On her faintly inquiring the occasion of this outrage, she was informed that one of her unwelcome visitors was an attorney and the other his client, who had thus, with as little decency as humanity, forced themselves into the chamber of an almost expiring woman. The motive of this intrusion was to demand her appearance, as a witness, in *a suit pending against her brother*, in which these men were parties concerned. No entreaties could prevail on them to quit the chamber, where they both remained, questioning, in a manner the most unfeeling and insulting, the unfortunate victim of their audacity and persecution. One of them, the client, with a barbarous and unmanly sneer, turning to his confederate, asked, "Who, to see the lady they were now speaking to, could believe that she had once been called the *beautiful* Mrs. Robinson?" To this he added other observations not less savage and brutal; and, after throwing on the bed a subpoena, quitted the apartment. The wretch who could thus, by insulting the sick, and violating every law of humanity and common decency, disgrace the figure of a man, was a *professor* and a *priest* of that religion which enjoins us– "not to break the bruised reed," *"and to bind up the broken in heart!"* His name shall be suppressed, through respect to the order of which he is an unworthy member. The consequences of this brutality upon the poor invalid were violent convulsions, which had nearly extinguished the struggling spark of life.

By slow degrees her malady yielded to the cares and skill of her medical attendants, and she was once more restored to temporary convalescence; but from that time her strength gradually decayed. Though her frame was shaken to its centre her circumstances compelled her still to exert the faculties of her mind.

The sportive exercises of fancy were now converted into toilsome labours of the brain–nights of sleepless anxiety were succeeded by days of vexation and dread.

About this period she was induced to undertake the poetical department for the editor of a morning paper, [1] and actually commenced a series of satirical odes, on local and temporary subjects, to which was affixed the signature of "Tabitha Bramble." Among these lighter compositions, considered by the author as unworthy of a place with her collected poems, a more matured production of her genius was occasionally introduced, of which the following "Ode to Spring," written April 30, 1780, is a beautiful and affecting example:

ODE TO SPRING.

Life-glowing season! odour-breathing Spring!
Deck'd in cerulean splendours!–vivid,–warm,
Shedding soft lustre on the rosy hours,
And calling forth their beauties! balmy Spring!
To thee the vegetating world begins
To pay fresh homage. Ev'ry southern gale
Whispers thy coming;–every tepid show'r
Revivifies thy charms. The mountain breeze
Wafts the ethereal essence to the vale,
While the low vale returns its fragrant hoard
With tenfold sweetness. When the dawn unfolds
Its purple splendours 'mid the dappled clouds,
Thy influence cheers the soul. When noon uplifts
Its burning canopy, spreading the plain
Of heaven's own radiance with one vast of light,
Thou smil'st triumphant! Ev'ry little flow'r

Seems to exult in thee, delicious Spring,
Luxuriant nurse of nature! By the stream,
That winds its swift course down the mountain's side,
Thy progeny are seen;–young primroses,
And all the varying buds of wildest birth,
Dotting the green slope gaily. On the thorn,
Which arms the hedge-row, the young birds invite
With merry minstrelsy, shrilly and maz'd
With winding cadences; now quick, now sunk
In the low twittered song. The evening sky
Reddens the distant main; catching the sail,
Which slowly lessens, and with crimson hue
Varying the sea-green wave; while the young moon,
Scarce visible amid the warmer tints
Of western splendours, slowly lifts her brow
Modest and icy-lustred! O'er the plain
The light dews rise, sprinkling the thistle's head,
And hanging its clear drops on the wild waste
Of broomy fragrance. Season of delight!
Thou soul-expanding pow'r, whose wondrous glow
Can bid all nature smile! Ah! why to me
Come unregarded, undelighting still
This ever-mourning bosom? So I've seen
The sweetest flow'rets bind the icy urn;
The brightest sunbeams glitter on the grave;
And the soft zephyr kiss the troubled main,
With whispered murmurs. Yes, to me, O Spring!
Thou com'st unwelcom'd by a smile of joy;
To me! slow with'ring to that silent grave
Where all is blank and dreary! Yet once more
The Spring eternal of the soul shall dawn,
Unvisited by clouds, by storms, by change,
Radiant and unexhausted! Then, ye buds,
Ye plumy minstrels, and ye balmy gales,
Adorn your little hour, and give your joys
To bless the fond world-loving traveller,
Who, smiling, measures the long flow'ry path
That leads to death! For to such wanderers

Life is a busy, pleasing, cheerful dream,
And the last hour unwelcome. Not to me,
O! not to me, stern Death, art thou a foe;
Thou art the welcome messenger, which brings
A passport to a blest and long repose

A just value was at that time set upon the exertions of Mrs. Robinson by the conductors of the paper, who "considered them as one of the principal embellishments and supports of their journal."

In the spring of 1800 she was compelled by the daily encroachments of her malady wholly to relinquish her literary employments.

Her disorder was pronounced by the physicians to be a rapid decline. Dr. Henry Vaughan, who to medical skill unites the most exalted philanthropy, prescribed, as a last resource, a journey to Bristol Wells. A desire once again to behold her native scenes induced Mrs. Robinson eagerly to accede to this proposal. She wept with melancholy pleasure at the idea of closing her eyes for ever upon a world of vanity and disappointment in the place in which she had first drawn breath, and terminating her sorrows on the spot which gave her birth; but even this sad solace was denied to her from a want of the pecuniary means for its execution. In vain she applied to those on whom honour, humanity, and justice, gave her undoubted claims. She even condescended to entreat, as a *donation* the return of those sums granted as a *loan* in her prosperity.

The following is a copy of a letter addressed on this occasion to a *noble* debtor, and found among the papers of Mrs. Robinson after her decease:

"TO –

" *April* 23, 1800.

"MY LORD,–Pronounced by my physicians to be in a rapid decline, I trust that your lordship will have the goodness to assist me with a part of the sum for which you are indebted to me. Without your aid I cannot make trial of the Bristol waters, the only remedy that presents to me any hope of preserving my existence. I should be sorry to die at enmity with any person; and you may be assured, my dear lord, that I bear none towards you. It would be useless to ask you to call on me; but if you would do me that honour, I should be happy, very happy, to see you, being,

"My dear lord,
"Yours truly,
"MARY ROBINSON.

To this letter no answer was returned!! Farther comments are unnecessary.

The last literary performance of Mrs. Robinson was a volume of Lyrical Tales. She repaired a short time after to a small cottage *ornée* belonging to her daughter, near Windsor. Rural occupation and amusement, quiet and pure air, appeared for a time to cheer her spirits and renovate her shattered frame. Once more her active mind returned to its accustomed and favourite pursuits; but the toil of supplying the constant variety required by a daily print, added to other engagements, which she almost despaired of being capacitated to fulfil, pressed heavily upon her spirits, and weighed down her enfeebled frame. Yet, in the month of August, she began and concluded, in the course of ten days, a translation of Dr. Hager's "Picture of Palermo"–an exertion by which she was greatly debilitated. She was compelled, though with reluctance, to relinquish the translation of "The Messiah" of Klopstock, which she had proposed giving to the English reader in blank verse–a task particularly suited to her genius and the turn of her mind.

But, amidst the pressure of complicated distress, the mind of this unfortunate woman was superior to improper concessions, and treated with just indignation those offers of service which required the sacrifice of her integrity.

She yet continued, though with difficulty and many intervals, her literary avocations. When necessitated by pain and languor to limit her exertions, her unfeeling employers accused her of negligence. This inconsideration, though she seldom complained, affected her spirits and preyed upon her heart. As she hourly declined towards that asylum where "the weary rest," her mind seemed to acquire strength in proportion to the weakness of her frame. When no longer able to support the fatigue of being removed from her chamber, she retained a perfect composure of spirits, and, in the intervals of extreme bodily suffering, would listen while her daughter read to her, with apparent interest and collectedness of thought, frequently making observations on what would probably take place when she had passed that "bourn whence no traveller returns." The flattering nature of her disorder at times inspired her friends with the most sanguine hopes of her restoration to health; she would even herself, at intervals, cherish the idea. But these gleams of hope, like flashes of lightning athwart the storm, were succeeded by a deeper gloom, and the consciousness of her approaching fate returned upon the mind of the sufferer with increased conviction.

Within a few days of her decease she collected and arranged her poetical works, which she bound her daughter, by a solemn adjuration, to publish for her subscribers, and also the present Memoir. Requesting earnestly that the papers prepared for the latter purpose might be brought to her, she gave them into the hands of Miss Robinson, with an injunction that the narrative should be made public, adding, "I should have continued it up to the present time–but perhaps it is as well that I have been prevented. Promise me that you will print it!" The request of a dying parent, so made, and at such a moment, could not be refused. She is obeyed. Upon the solemn assurances of her daughter, that her last desire so strongly urged should be complied with, the mind of Mrs. Robinson became composed and tranquil; her intellects yet remained unimpaired, though her corporeal strength hourly decayed.

A short time previous to her death, during an interval of her daughter's absence from her chamber, she called an attending friend, whose benevolent heart and unremitting kindness will, it is hoped, meet hereafter with their reward, and entreated her to observe her last requests, adding, with melancholy tenderness, "I cannot talk to my poor girl on these sad subjects." Then, with an unruffled manner and minute precision, she gave orders respecting her interment, which she desired might be performed with all possible simplicity. "Let me," said she, with an impressive though almost inarticulate voice, "be buried in Old Windsor churchyard." For the selection of that spot she gave. She *a particular reason,* also mentioned an undertaker, whose name she recollected having seen on his door, and whom she appointed from his vicinity to the probable place of her decease. A few trifling memorials, as tributes of her affection, were all the property she had to bequeath. She also earnestly desired that a part of her hair might be sent to two *particular persons.*

One evening, her anxious nurses, with a view to divert her mind, talked of some little plans to take place on her restoration to health. She shook her head with an affecting and significant motion. "Don't deceive yourselves," said she; "remember, I tell you, I am but a very little time longer for this world." Then pressing to her heart her daughter, who knelt by her bedside, she held her head for some minutes clasped against her bosom, which throbbed, as with some internal and agonising conflict. "Poor heart," murmured she, in a deep and stifled tone, what will become of thee!" She paused some moments, and at length struggling to assume more composure, desired in a calmer voice that some one would read to her. Throughout the remainder of the evening she continued placidly and even cheerfully attentive to the person who read, observing that, *should* she recover, she designed to commence a long work, upon which she would bestow great pains and time. "Most of her writings," she added, "had been composed in too much haste."

Her disorder rapidly drawing towards a period, the accumulation of the water upon her chest every moment threatened suffocation.

For nearly fifteen nights and days she was obliged to be supported upon pillows, or in the arms of her young and affectionate nurses. [1] Her decease, through this period, was hourly expected. On the 24th of December she inquired how near was Christmas Day! Being answered, "Within a few days " *Yet*"– said she, "I shall never see it." The remainder of this melancholy day passed in undescribable tortures. Towards midnight, the sufferer exclaimed, "O God, O just and merciful God, help me to support this agony!" The whole of the ensuing day she continued to endure great anguish. In the evening a kind of lethargic stupor came on. Miss Robinson, approaching the pillow of her expiring mother, earnestly conjured her to speak, if in her power. "My darling Mary!" she faintly articulated, and spoke no more. In another hour she became insensible to the grief of those by whom she was surrounded, and breathed her last at a quarter past twelve on the following noon.

The body was opened, at the express wish of Drs. Pope and Chandler. The immediate cause of her death appeared to have been a dropsy on the chest; but the sufferings which she endured previously to her decease were probably occasioned by six large gall-stones found in the gall-bladder.

All her requests were strictly observed. Her remains were deposited, according to her direction, in the churchyard of Old Windsor; the spot was marked out by a friend to whom she had signified her wishes. The funeral was attended only by two literary friends.

Respecting the circumstances of the preceding narrative, every reader must be left to form his own reflections. To the humane mind, the errors of the unfortunate subject of this Memoir will appear to have been more than expiated by her sufferings. Nor will the peculiar disadvantages by which her introduction into life was attended, be forgotten by the candid–disadvantages that, by converting into a snare the bounties lavished on her by nature, proved not less fatal to her happiness than to her conduct. On her unhappy marriage, and its still more unhappy consequences, it is unnecessary to comment. Thus circumstanced, her genius, her sensibility, and her beauty combined to her destruction, while, by her exposed situation, her inexperience of life, her tender youth, with the magnitude of the temptations which beset her, she could scarcely fail of being betrayed.

> "Say, ye severest–
> –what would you have done?"

The malady which seized her in the bloom of youth, and pursued her with unmitigable severity through every stage of life, till, in the prime of her powers, it laid her in a premature grave, exhibits, in the history of its progress, a series of sufferings that might disarm the sternest, soften the most rigid, and awaken pity in the hardest heart. Her mental exertions through this depressing disease, the elasticity of her mind and the perseverance of her efforts amidst numberless sources of vexation and distress, cannot fail, while they awaken sympathy, to extort admiration. Had this lovely plant, now withered and low in the dust, been in its early growth transplanted into a happier soil–sheltered from the keen blasts of adversity, and the mildew of detraction, it might have extended its roots, unfolded its blossoms, diffused its sweetness, shed its perfumes, and still flourished, beauteous to the eye, and grateful to the sense.

To represent the character of the individual in the circumstances of life, his conduct under those circumstances, and the consequences which they ultimately produce, is the peculiar province of biography. Little therefore remains to be added. The benevolent temper, the filial piety, and the maternal tenderness of Mrs. Robinson are exemplified in the preceding pages, as her genius, her talents, the fertility of her imagination and the powers of her mind are displayed in her productions, the popularity of which at least affords a presumption of their merit. Her manners were polished and conciliating, her powers of conversation rich and varied. The brilliancy of her wit and the sallies of her fancy were ever tempered by kindness and chastened by delicacy. Though accustomed to the society of the great, and paying to rank the tribute which civil institutions have rendered its due, she reserved her esteem and deference for those only whose talents or whose merits claimed the homage of the mind.

With the unfortunate votaries of letters she sincerely sympathised, and not unfrequently has been known to divide the profits of her genius with the less successful or less favoured disciples of the muse.

The productions of Mrs. Robinson, both in prose and verse, are numerous, and of various degrees of merit; but to poetry the native impulse of her genius appears to have been more peculiarly directed. Of the glitter and false taste exhibited in the *Della Crusca* correspondence [1] she became early sensible; several of her poems breathe a spirit of just sentiment and simple elegance.

A PASTORAL ELEGY

ON

THE DEATH OF MRS. ROBINSON,

[BY PETER PINDAR]

FAREWELL to the nymph of my heart!
Farewell to the cottage and vine!
From *these* with a tear, I depart,
Where pleasure so often was *mine.*

Remembrance shall dwell on her smile,
And dwell on her lute and her song;
That sweetly my hours to beguile,
Oft echoed the valleys along.

Once more the fair scene let me view,
The grotto, the brook, and the grove
Dear valleys, for ever adieu!
Adieu to the DAUGHTER of LOVE!

FOOTNOTES

[1] Collin's Peerage gives the following account of this lady: "Peter, Lord King married Anne, daughter of Richard Seys, Esq., of Boverton, in Glamorganshire, with whom he lived to the day of his death in perfect love and happiness, and left by her four sons and two daughters" (vol. vii. p. 273).

[1] A portrait of my grandmother, when a girl, was seen by my mother at Haswell, in Somersetshire, the seat of Sir C. K. Tynt, many years after I was born.

[1] I may with truth, and without vanity, make this remark. The estimable being here mentioned was named John; he died on the 7th of December, 1790, at Leghorn, in Tuscany, where he had been many years established as a merchant of the first respectability.

[1] Hannah More, with her sisters, at this time kept a boarding-school for young ladies. Later she became famous as the author of tragedies which gained popularity.–ED.

[1] Mr. Powel.

[1] Thomas Hull, deputy manager of Covent Garden Theatre, was founder of the Theatrical Fund for the relief of distressed players. He was an actor, the author and translator of several plays, and a writer of poems and short stories.–ED.

[2] David Garrick, the famous actor and manager of Drury Lane Theatre, made his last appearance on the stage on the 10th of June, 1776, he being then in his sixtieth year.–ED

[3] Arthur Murphy, an Irishman, began life as a clerk, then became a journalist and subsequently an actor, but remaining on the stage only for a couple of seasons, he turned dramatist and wrote a number of plays, some of which attained great success. Two years

after the death of David Garrick he wrote a life of the famous player, who had been his intimate friend.–ED

[1] Susannah Cibber, who gained considerable fame as a singer in oratorio before becoming an acress. Her first success as a player was gained at Covent Garden, but in 1753 she joined Garrick's company at Drury Lane, of which she remained a member until her death in 1766. Garrick, who greatly admired her genius, on hearing of her demise, declared, "Then tragedy is dead on one side." She lies buried in Westminster Abbey.

[1] At the time when the banns of her marriage were published she admits to being "a few months advanced in her sixteenth year"; and she had been four months married when the journey to Bristol was made.–ED.

[1] Mrs. Sophia Baddeley, Who was a very beautiful woman, and the heroine of many amorous adventures.–ED.

[1] Robert Henley, who, in 1772, succeeded his father as second Earl of Northington. Previous to this date he had been made an LL.D. of Cambridge, and had held the offices of Teller of the Exchequer, and Master of the Hanaper Office in Chancery. The year after his succession he was made Knight of the Thistle, and in 1783 was appointed Lord-Lieutenant of Ireland.–ED.

[1] Thomas, second Baron Lyttelton, known as "the wicked Lord Lyttelton," in distinction to his father, who in his lifetime had been styled "the good Lord Lyttelton." Thomas, Baron Lyttelton, was a man of parts and fashion; a politician, a writer of verses, an artist whose paintings were supposed to contain the combined excellencies of Salvator Rosa and Claude, and withal one of the greatest profligates of the age. This is the Lord Lyttelton who, in his thirty-fifth year, and whilst in perfect health, dreamt a woman appeared to him and announced he had not three days to live. He spoke lightly of his dream, and on the morning of the third day felt in such good spirits that he declared he should "bilk the ghost." He died suddenly

that night, when his friend Miles Peter Andrews dreamt Lyttelton appeared to him and said, "All is over."

George Edward Ayscough a captain in the Guards, was cousin to the second Lord Lyttelton. Some years later than the date of his meeting with Mrs. Robinson he produced a version of Voltaire's "Semiramis," which was presented at Drury Lane Theatre in 1776. He is described as "a parasite of Lord Lyttelton," and as "a fool of fashion."–ED.

[1] Anna Lætitia Aikin (1743-1825).–ED.

[1] George Robert Fitzgerald, commonly known as "Fighting Fitzgerald," from the number of duels in which he took part, was a man of good family, noted alike for his gallantry and recklessness. A fracas which was the result of his distasteful attentions to Mrs. Hartley, a well-known actress, had made him notorious in 1773, some years previous to his introduction to Mrs. Robinson. His life, which was one of singular adventure, ended on the scaffold, he being executed for murder in 1786.–ED

[1] Mrs. Abington, a distinguished actress who, at the age of seventeen, had made her first appearance at the Haymarket Theatre, some six years before the author of these memoirs was born.

[1] Later she gave birth to a daughter named Sophia, who lived but six weeks.–ED.

[1] Mr. Robinson was educated at Harrow, and was a contemporary of Mr. Sheridan.

[1] This gentleman's name is Hanway, the person mentioned in the former part of this work, as Mr. Robinson's earliest friend.

[1] Writing of this time, Miss Hawkins states that Mrs. Robinson was "eminently meritorious: she had her child to attend to, she did all the work of their apartments, she even scoured the stairs, and accepted the writing and the pay Which he had refused."–ED.

[1] Georgiana, wife of the fifth Duke of Devonshire. The Duchess was not only one of the most beautiful, vivacious, and fascinating women of the day, but was likewise an ardent politician. Whilst canvassing for the election of Fox she purchased the vote of a butcher for a kiss, and received from an Irish mechanic the complimentary assurance that he could light his pipe at her eyes.–ED.

[1] George Hobart, third Earl of Buckinghamshire, who had a passion for dramatic entertainments, and for a time became manager of the opera in London.–ED.

[1] Richard Brinsley Sheridan was at this period in his twenty-fifth year, and had entered on his mismanagement of Drury Lane Theatre. He had already written The Rivals, which had not proved a success on its first appearance; St. Patrick's Day, or the Scheming Lieutenant, a farce; The Duenna, a comic opera; but he was yet to write A Trip to Scarborough, and The School for Scandal.

[1] In his "History of the Stage," Genest tells us Mrs. Robinson made her first appearance on the stage as Juliet on the 10th of December, 1776, but leaves us in ignorance regarding the actors who took part in the tragedy. Romeo was evidently played by William Brereton, who had rehearsed the principal scenes with her in the green- room before Sheridan and Garrick. Genest adds: "Mrs. Robinson was received with great applause. She had an engagement previous to her first appearance, and received what was considered a handsome salary. She was a most beautiful woman, and a very good breeches figure"–ED.

[1] According to Genest, the second character she attempted was Statira, in Alexander the Great, played on the 17th of February, 1777; Amanda, in The Trip to Scarborough, produced seven nights later, being her third personation.–ED.

[2] Ernest Augustus Duke of Cumberland, and afterwards King of Hanover, was the fifth son of George III., and perhaps the most profligate and unpopular member of the royal family.–ED.

[1] Horace Walpole, writing to his friend, the Rev. William Mason, on the 28th of May, 1780, says: "Lady Craven's comedy, called The Miniature Picture, which she acted herself with a genteel set at her own house in the country, has been played at Drury Lane. The chief singularity was that she went to it herself the second night in form; sat in the middle of the front row of the stage box, much dressed with a profusion of white bugles and plumes, to receive the public homage due to her sex and loveliness.... It was amazing to see so young a woman entirely possess herself; but there is such an integrity and frankness in her consciousness of her own beauty and talents, that she speaks of them with a as if she had no property in them, but only wore them as gifts of the gods. Lord Craven, on the contrary, was quite agitated by his fondness for her, and with impatience at the bad performance of the actors, which was wretched indeed. Yet the address of the plot, which is the chief merit of the piece, and some lively pencilling, carried it off very well, though Parsons murdered the Scotch Lord, and Mrs. Robinson (who is supposed to be the favourite of the Prince of Wales) thought on nothing but her own charms and him."

The Irish Widow was a farce founded by David Garrick on Molière's Le Mariage Forcé, and produced on the 23rd of October, 1772.–ED.

[1] Thomas Linley, who was considered "one of the finest violin players in Europe," was drowned through the upsetting of a boat on the 5th of August, 1778. He was a brother-in-law of Richard Brinsley Sheridan.–ED

[2] George Colman, a popular and prolific dramatist, who in 1727 became manager of the Haymarket Theatre, and continued as such until 1785, introducing meansvhile many new players and some dramatic novelties.–ED.

[1] Elizabeth Farren, born 1759, made her first appearance before a London audience as Miss Hardcastle in She Stoops to Conquer, on June 9, 1777 . After years spent in strolling through the provinces in her father's company and that of other managers, she now captivated the town. Her beautiful face, exquisitely modulated voice,

elegant figure, and natural grace, rendered her an ideal representative of the fine ladies of comedy. She was welcomed into the most distinguished society in London, and whilst acting as manageress of private theatricals at the Duke of Richmond's house in Whitehall, met Edward, twelfth Earl of Derby, whose wife was then living. This did not prevent him from falling in love with Miss Farren, who, it was understood, would succeed his first wife as countess did the latter predecease the actress. Lady Derby died on March 14, 1797, and on the 8th of the following month Miss Farren took leave of the stage in the character of Lady Teazle, and on the 1st of May was married to Lord Derby, she being then in her thirty-eighth year. Even in this scandal-loving and licentious age no imputation had ever been cast upon her honour. Of the three children born of this union but one survived, a daughter, who married the Earl of Wilton. The Countess of Derby lived until 1829.–ED.

[1] Mrs. Robinson played Lady Macbeth on the occasion of her benefit, when was also performed a musical farce she had composed entitled A Lucky Escape.–ED

[1] The famous politician Charles James Fox, a friend of the Prince of Wales.–ED.

[1] George III. and Queen Charlotte, who frequently attended the theatre.–ED.

[1] This performance of The Winter's Tale took place on December 3, 1779, she being at that time in her twenty-second year, and the Prince of Wales in his eighteenth year.–ED.

[2] Smith had been educated at Eton and St. John's College, Cambridge, with a view to becoming a clergyman, but eventually went on the stage and proved himself an excellent actor, whose representation of Charles Surface was considered a finished performance.–ED

[3] George Capel Coningsby, Viscount Maiden, after- wards fifth Earl of Essex, born November 13, 1757. He married twice, his second wife being Miss Stephens, the famous singer.–ED.

[1] Those who have read The Winter's Tale will know the significance of these adopted names.

[1] The writer evidently makes a mistake in fixing the Oratorio for the next night, as will be seen from the note on the next page.–ED.

[1] Frederick Augustus, Duke of York and Albany, second son of George III., who at the age of six months was elected to the valuable bishopric of Osnaburg.–ED.

[1] Another of the "diurnal prints" dated February 12, 1780, is not so complimentary in its remarks, which run as follows: "A circumstance of rather an embarrassing nature happened at last night's Oratorio. Mrs. R–, decked out in all her finery, took care to post herself in one of the upper boxes immediately opposite the Prince's, and by those airs peculiar to herself, contrived at last so to a certain Heir-apparent, that his fixed attention to the beautiful object above became generally noticed, and soon after astonished their Majesties, who, not being able to discover the cause, seemed at a loss to account for the extraordinary effect. No sooner, however, were they properly informed than a messenger was instantly sent aloft desiring the dart-dealing actress to withdraw, which she complied with, though not without expressing the utmost chagrin at her mortifying removal."–ED.

[1] At this time the Prince of Wales and his brother Frederick Augustus, Duke of York, were living in seclusion at Boner Lodge, Kew, where their education was being conducted by Dr. Hurd, Bishop of Lichfield, Mr. Arnold, and Lord Bruce. A strict discipline was exercised over the princes at this period. It was not until January 1, 1781, that the Prince of Wales was provided with a separate establishment, a part of Buckingham House being allotted to him for that purpose–ED.

[1] Now Margravine of Anspach.

[1] The most affecting tribute which the memory of a gallant father could receive was the following pathetic and heartfelt effusion of genuine and grateful duty:

TO THE

MEMORY

OF

MY LAMENTED FATHER,

WHO DIED IN THE SERVICE OF THE EMPRESS OF RUSSIA,

DECEMBER 5, 1786

Oh, sire, rever'd! ador'd!
Was it the ruthless tongue of DEATH,
  That whisp'ring to my pensive ear,
  Pronounc'd the fatal word
  That bath'd my cheek with many a tear,
And stopp'd awhile my gasping breath?
  ' He lives no more!
  Far on a foreign shore,
His honour'd dust a laurell'd grave receives,
While his immortal soul in realms celestial lives! '

Oh! my lov'd sire, farewell!
Though we are doom'd on earth to meet no more,
Still mem'ry lives, and still I must adore!
And long this throbbing heart shall mourn,
Though thou to these sad eyes wilt ne'er return!
  Yet shall remembrance dwell
  On all thy sorrows through life's stormy sea,
When fate's resistless whirlwinds shed

Unnumber'd tempests round thy head,
  The varying ills of human destiny!

Yet, with a soul sublimely brave,
Didst thou endure the dashing wave;
Still buffeting the billows rude,
By all the shafts of woe, undaunted, unsubdued!
  Through a long life of rugged care,
'Twas thine to steer a steady course!
  'Twas thine misfortune's frowns to bear,
And stem the wayward torrent's force!
  And as thy persevering mind
The toilsome path of fame pursued,
  'Twas thine, amidst its flow'rs to find
The wily snake–Ingratitude!
  Yet vainly did th' insidious reptile strive
On thee its poisons dire to fling;
  Above its reach, thy laurel still shall thrive,
Unconscious of the treach'rous sting!

'Twas thine to toil through length'ning years,
Where low'ring night absorbs the spheres!
  O'er icy seas to bend thy way,
Where frozen Greenland rears its head,
  Where dusky vapours shroud the day,
And wastes of flaky snow the stagnate ocean spread
  'Twas thine amidst the smoke of war,
  To view, unmov'd, grim-fronted Death;
  Where Fate, enthron'd in sulphur'd car,
Shrunk the pale legions with her scorching breath!
  While all around her, bath'd in blood,
Iberia's haughty sons plung'd lifeless 'midst the flood.

  Now on the wings of meditation borne,
Let fond remembrance turn, and turn to mourn;
Slowly, and sad, her pinions sweep
O'er the rough bosom of the boist'rous deep
  To that disastrous, fatal coast

Where, on the foaming billows tost,
Imperial Catherine's navies rode;
  And war's inviting banners wide
  Wav'd hostile o'er the glitt'ring tide,
That with exulting conquest glow'd!

  For there—oh sorrow, check the tear!–
  There, round departed valour's bier,
The sacred drops of kindred virtue [1] shone!
  Proud monuments of worth! whose base
  Fame on her starry hill shall place;
  There to endure, admir'd, sublime!
  E'en when the mould'ring wing of time
Shall scatter to the winds huge pyramids of stone!
  Oh! gallant soul! farewell!
Though doom'd this transient orb to leave,
  Thy daughter's heart, whose grief no words can tell
Shall, in its throbbing centre, bid thee live!
  While from its crimson fount shall flow
The silent tear of ling'ring grief;
The gem sublime! that scorns relief,
  Nor vaunting shines, with ostentatious woe!

Though thou art vanish'd from these eyes,
Still from thy sacred dust shall rise
  A wreath that mocks the polish'd grace
Of sculptured bust, or tuneful praise;
  While Fame shall weeping point the place
Where Valour's dauntless son decays!
Unseen to cherish mem'ry's source divine,
Oh! parent of my life, shall still be mine!

  And thou shalt, from thy blissful state,
  Awhile avert thy raptur'd gaze,
To own, that 'midst this wild'ring maze,
  The flame of filial love defies the blast of fate!

[1] Captain Darby commanded, at the time of his death, a ship of war in the Russian service, and was buried with military honours, universally lamented.

[1] Dumouriez.

[1] An attachment took place between Mrs. Robinson and Colonel Tarleton shortly after the return of the latter from America, which subsisted during sixteen years. On the circumstances which occasioned its dissolution it is neither necessary nor would it be proper to dwell. The exertions of Mrs. Robinson in the service of Colonel Tarleton, when pressed by pecuniary embarrassment, led to that unfortunate journey, the consequences of which proved so fatal to her health. The colonel accompanied her to the Continent, and, by his affectionate attentions, sought to alleviate those sufferings of which he had been the involuntary occasion.

[1] Son of the celebrated Edmund Burke.

[1] The Right Honourable Edmund Burke, at that time conductor of the Annual Register.

[1] Mr. Merry had been a member of the "Scuola della Crusca," at Florence

[1] Mrs. Robinson's "Poems," vol. ii. p. 27.

[1] The date on which the Paris prisons were broken open and twelve hundred royalist prisoners slain–ED.

[1] Boaden, in his Life of Kemble, says: "I remember the warmth with which Mrs. Robinson chanted the kindness of Mrs. Jordan in accepting the principal character: and I cannot forget the way, when the storm began, in which the actress, frightened out of her senses, 'died and made no sign.'"–ED.

[1] 1 *The Morning Post.*

[1] Miss Robinson and a friend.

[1] Those who have read Gifford's "Baviad" and "Mæviad" will understand this allusion–ED.

CPSIA information can be obtained at www.ICGtesting.com
Printed in the USA
BVOW022251280812

299034BV00002B/91/P